DESTROYING DEMONIC HOUSES

Understanding and Pulling Down Strongholds

Spiritual Warfare 4

I0138370

George Rwizi

DEDICATION

I wouldn't be where I am without a supportive family. My beautiful wife, Love (Rudo) is a tremendous, supportive pillar in all I do. Not to mention my lovely daughters, Kundai, Kudzai and Kunashe. Ezekiel Guti Jnr, our very long relationship and your allowing yourself to be a son to us has, over the years proved to be very inspirational to me and I cherish it. I dedicate this life-changing treatise to you guys. God bless you.

ACKNOWLEDGEMENTS

I want to acknowledge the mentorship of my spiritual parents, Archbishop Ezekiel and Eunor Guti and their tireless effort in bringing me up. Your influence over my life is engraved and remains indelible until we get to the other side of eternity. I love you Mom and Dad. Dr. Jeana Tomlinson, I thank God you are my father's spiritual daughter. God bless you for all the effort you put in editing the raw manuscript. Thank you Pastor Love River for helping with the editing. I acknowledge my mother-in-law, Pastor Pheobe Kahwema and my Dad, Amos Rwizi, for their tireless intercessory ministry for us as a family and for all we do in the work of the ministry.

FOREWORD 1

"I will no longer talk much with you, for the ruler of this world is coming and he has nothing in Me".

This statement was said by Jesus Christ to His disciples as recorded in John 14:30, immediately before His arrest by a detachment of troops at the instigation of the chief priests and the Pharisees. The statement said by Jesus seemed to suggest that if there was something to the liking of the ruler of this world in Jesus, he could have had his way.

It is very interesting as one notices the fact that the Lord Jesus Christ associated the coming of the ruler of this world, who of course is the Devil, to attack Him with His spiritual condition. The phrase "he has nothing in Me" gives an insight into the suggested spiritual condition of Jesus. As if Jesus had examined Himself in order to establish and understand if there were any strongholds or weaknesses in Him for the ruler of this world to hang on to and torment the Lord from that position, Jesus said there were no such strongholds, demonic houses or weakness in Him.

Could it be that by indicating that there was nothing in Him for the ruler of this world, Jesus Christ was also showing that the possibility for such strongholds to be in Him was there? Could it be that He also had the need to pull down and demolish such strong holds if there were any? Why would the Lord Jesus Christ find it necessary to inform His disciples that there was nothing in Him for the ruler of this world if there was no need for Him to also pull down and demolish such strongholds?

In this book, George Rwizi, with tact, simplicity, clarity and illumination exposes scriptural strongholds as demonic houses or one's weaknesses where demons can be housed. From there these demons will make sure that these houses are always producing their intended results. As much, the author explicitly warns that there is a need for pulling down and destroying these demonic houses in order a Christian to thoroughly enjoy and maintain his deliverance.

The book goes on to beautifully provide the method that one can use in pulling down these strongholds and destroying them completely as the author writes, "I want to submit to you that the problem is not only lack of knowledge or lack of opportunities to learn but the need for "unlearning" the wrong knowledge we learnt over the years. In a way pulling down strongholds or demolishing strongholds becomes synonymous to this "unlearning" process. We have established that we pull down strongholds by besieging our minds with the truth but the truth will be helpless before this unlearning process is complete.

The author goes further to show us that pulling down strongholds is synonymous to the renewing of our minds. The word besieging used above is a military term which gives the idea of invading and capturing a fortified location in order to bring it under control and authority of the besieger. The process of besieging our minds with the truth, gives the idea of invading and capturing our minds with the truth, bringing every thought into captivity to the obedience of Christ, (2 Corinthians 10-5).

On the other hand, the Word of God which is our strongest weapon in this process is capacitated to discern the thoughts and intentions of our minds, (Hebrew 4:12). As such, we are capacitated therefore, able to pull down strongholds, casting down arguments and every high thing that exalts itself against the knowledge of God.

Basically the pulling down of strongholds or demonic houses and their total destruction is centered around our mind as evidenced by the fact that we need to acquire correct knowledge and in that process there is a need for unlearning the wrong knowledge first which we learnt over the years. We are further informed that the pulling down of strongholds is synonymous to renewing one's mind.

This whole process shows us that one way or the other, we have to engage our minds in order for us to be successful in our efforts to pull down these demonic houses and destroy them completely. For this reason, the Bible has this to say, "keep thy heart with all diligence, for out of it are the issues of life" (Proverbs 4; 23 KJV). According to this scripture and many others, all issues or matters of our lives proceed from our heart. Some of the few issues of our lives could be social, emotional, physical, spiritual, material, financial, professional, academic, health and many others. The Bible says all these proceed from our heart, hence the need to keep our heart with all diligence.

It should be noted and understood that the bible heart being discussed here is our mindset and not the biological organ found in our chest which pumps our blood. In fact, the bible heart is our mind.

Notice what Hebrews 4:12 says as it reads,

"for the word of God is quick and powerful, and sharper than any two double edged sword, piercing even to the dividing of the soul and spirit and of the joints and marrow and is a discerner of the thoughts and intents of the heart."

Here the phrase "thoughts and intents of the heart" shows us that the bible heart is made of thoughts and intentions. In Matthew 15:19 Jesus said "for out of the heart, come forth evil thoughts." It is common knowledge that our thoughts proceed from our mind. Of course, our mind exists in our brain which is in our head. Therefore, when the Bible admonishes us to keep our heart, it is admonishing us to guard our mind with all diligence since the issues or matters of our lives proceed from our mind.

In this book, not only did the author receive an illumination from the Holy Spirit, there was a need for unlearning the wrong knowledge first we acquired over the years and then obtain correct knowledge but also emphasized the fact that if this was done, enjoyment and maintenance of one's deliverance could be guaranteed. Preachers, evangelists and those who need deliverance and those who operate in the ministry of deliverance are guaranteed of a good and useable tool in this book.

It's very informative, educative, empowering and it's a good book to read. Furthermore, the approach the Pastor George preferred in it leaves it without a rival. I can keep a copy in my library.

Dr. Jason Marowa
Chaplain General (Rtd)
Zimbabwe Republic Police

FOREWORD 2

I have known Pastor George Rwizi for many years. We share the same spiritual parentage.

Of course, I perused this work before I could comment on it and I found the content to be Biblically sound. That is the most important aspect to any Christian teaching. Can we find the direct correlation of the author's concepts reflected in Holy Scriptures? The burden of proof, actually, does not rest entirely on the shoulders of the author. We, the readers, have a mandate to "prove that which is good" – Romans 12:2

My journey to follow Jesus and to become increasingly more acquainted with His Word has enabled me to detect renegade philosophies – not because I consider myself a scholar or theologian. I have an insatiable love for the Bible; therefore, if someone is sharing from their personal experiences but erring from the Word of God, an inner flag goes up. It is an internal "caution light" that clicks on because of a notion that does not line up with what God says. Anyone who loves the Bible possesses it. With this said it is an absolute joy to read the works of someone who is steady, obedient and FULL OF THE WORD!

Pastor George Rwizi and I are very familiar with demonic activity and how to appropriately deal with evil spirits. We run in the circles of those who have no hesitation in calling out and casting out demons. Not every Christian – not every church – is comfortable with the subject. But all of us have been instructed about the devil from the lips of the Savior. Dealing with evil can be devastating. Learning how to approach the subject requires skill, discernment, protection, caution and an anointing. All of these are available to anyone who desires to learn more.

In this study, Pastor George has taken a weighty subject that is overwhelming for many Christian and has broken it into bite-size pieces for even babes-in-Christ to comprehend and activate.

It is refreshing to learn something new especially when you think you have heard it all! I am not as old a Methuselah but I have been around for a while...

Destroying Demon Houses has opened my eyes to a new way of helping people. Knowing that I must first demolish the house that the evil spirits are living in has expanded my view of dealing more effectively with Satan.

You know the devil does not die. Jesus referred to him as "the god of this world". – 2 Corinthians 4:4

Knowing that he is a very present evil in this day, causes us to desire more fervently how to extricate his dark influence from the lives of those who have gone astray or, even, for those who love the Lord but have fallen into a snare/pit.

A stronghold is something in your life that you do not want but you cannot get rid of.

Pastor George will show you, step by step, how to demolish every stronghold that has entered into your life through various tricks of the devil. By the time you finish reading this most effective tutorial, you will have acquired all of the tools and skills available to live a life of true freedom. And that, My Friend, is worth the read

Dr. Jeana Tomlinson
New Covenant Ministries
Jacksonville, Florida

TABLE OF CONTENTS

INTRODUCTION

For years I really thought strongholds were demons. Every time I needed to deal with strongholds I would pray against demons. I had this erroneous concept in my mind that a stronghold was a strong, powerful and stubborn demon. Maybe there is someone out there who, like me, is of that opinion. Follow me in this book as I explain what strongholds are, how they are built, how they operate and how they can be pulled down effectively.

Usually the tendency is to confuse strongholds with the strongman our Lord Jesus Christ taught about in Matthew 12:29 where the Bible says,

"Or how can one enter a strong man's house and plunder his goods, unless he first binds the strong man? And then he will plunder his house."

It is essential, at this stage, to understand that strongholds are not demons. Remember in our study of curses (Spiritual warfare I) we established that curses are not demons but demons are assigned by the devil to orchestrate events in such a way that the curse is effective. Similarly strongholds are not demons but demons can be HOUSED in strongholds to maintain the strongholds and make them effective. The demon makes sure the stronghold is producing results. This is why I call strongholds DEMONIC HOUSES.

For example, a demon of poverty can be housed in a stronghold that says, "No one in my family or clan ever succeeds." The devil will then give that demon a simple instruction or assignment of making sure it hinders all forms of success. At the same time it fights hard to maintain the status quo. The demonic house must remain or it must be enforced. It is responsible for making repairs to that house. Whatever was used to build that stronghold must remain.

The story of Judas Iscariot is a typical example about demonic houses. Judas Iscariot had a stronghold that resulted in him stealing from the treasury belonging to Jesus' team. When Satan came looking for someone to fill so that he could betray Jesus, he came with an offer of a monetary reward and he came looking for someone with a money weakness or stronghold. He found Judas Iscariot. The stronghold in Judas became a demonic house.

Failure to deal with strongholds can be very catastrophic. Remember God destroyed the world because their imagination was evil. Genesis 6:5 says,

"Then the Lord saw that the wickedness of man was great in the earth, and that every intent of the thoughts of his heart was only evil continually."

Most cases of addiction are linked to strongholds and any attempt to free people from addictions without addressing the issue of strongholds can end up futile and frustrating as failure results. I will follow this up and give detail in a later chapter on Strongholds of addiction. Read on with open-mindedness and prayerfully. Like I said, I had a wrong view of what a stronghold was but I had to change my perspective after receiving new truth. Remember Hosea 4:6 says,

"My people are destroyed for lack of knowledge. Because you have rejected knowledge, I also will reject you from being priest for Me; Because you have forgotten the law of your God, I also will forget your children."

I want to submit to you that the problem is not only lack of knowledge or lack of opportunities to learn BUT the need for "unlearning" the wrong knowledge we learnt over the years. In a way, pulling down strongholds or demolishing strongholds becomes synonymous to this "unlearning" process. We have established that we pull down strongholds by besieging our minds with truth but that truth will be helpless before this unlearning process is complete. Romans 12:2 says,

"And do not be conformed to this world, but be transformed by the renewing of your mind, that you may prove what is that good and acceptable and perfect will of God."

In fact pulling down strongholds is synonymous to "the renewing of your mind" mentioned in Romans 12:2.

CHAPTER 1

WHAT IS A STRONGHOLD OR DEMONIC HOUSE?

An analysis of the appearance or mention of the word "stronghold" in the bible gives us a great clue into what a stronghold is. Of course "demonic house" is my own terminology. Did you hear that demon, in Matthew 12:43-45, saying, ".I will go back to my house.. " The Bible explains how Judas was a thief and he would often steal from the money bag since he was the treasurer in Jesus' crusade team. He had a "financial stronghold." Now, when Satan came looking for someone to enter so he could betray Jesus, he had to find someone who had a financial stronghold and offered him money. The financial stronghold became a demonic house. Remember I hinted on this in the introduction.

Before we get into the Word, it is necessary for us to define "stronghold" from an English perspective. A stronghold is a place that has been fortified so as to protect it against attack. It is sometimes called a fortress, fort, castle, citadel or garrison. It can also be defined as a place where a particular cause or belief is strongly defended or upheld, for example a political party's stronghold. One of the words the Thesaurus uses for stronghold is redoubt and it describes it as an entrenched stronghold or refuge. The thesaurus also uses these synonyms:

refuge, haven, retreat, hideout, and bulwark. It describes it as a strongly fortified defensive structure.

The Merriam-Webster dictionary defines it as a small building or area that gives protection to soldiers under attack or a safe or protected place, a secure retreat. The Free dictionary describes a stronghold as an area dominated or occupied by a special group or distinguished by a special quality. The Merriam-Webster dictionary adds that "a stronghold is a protected place where the members of a military group stay and can defend themselves."

One common thing we are getting from all the different English definitions and explanations is that a stronghold is strong. Actually, etymologically, strong-hold implies holding strong and, as we will see in the chapter dealing with "How to pull down strongholds", this is suggestive that pulling down a stronghold might not be an overnight chore. Essentially, a stronghold is described as a fortress with difficult access.

Now, turning to the Biblical viewpoint of a stronghold, it must be noted that the word occurs once in the New Testament and about 50 times in the Old Testament. The Greek word used there is "ochuroma or oxyroma" and it is translated a stronghold or fortress, a strong defence. It is a strong walled fortress. It is used figuratively of a false argument in which a person seeks shelter to escape reality. Strongholds are wrong thinking patterns that are contrary to the Word of God. They are strongly established sinful ways, false beliefs and behaviours. In areas that strongholds are established, an individual is either unable to consistently follow God's Word or unable to accept it because strongholds have an excessive influence on him or

A STRONGHOLD IS A PATTERN OF UNRIGHTEOUS THINKING THAT HOLDS THE VICTIM HOSTAGE OUTSIDE OF THE WILL OF GOD

her. Strongholds can be deeply implanted in the personality of a victim. Unless one desires to be delivered from them it can be difficult to deal with a person under the influence of a stronghold.

A stronghold is a pattern of unrighteous thinking that holds the victim hostage outside of the will of God. The victim is trapped in an addictive or negative life pattern. A stronghold is anything that exalts itself in our minds, pretending to be bigger or more powerful than God. God gets smaller and smaller in the victim's mind as the stronghold is reinforced and this causes the victim to feel overpowered, controlled and mastered.

Strongholds arise whenever we allow something to appear bigger than God. They come from false ideas. It is encouraging to remember that they are only lies and deceptions. However, we thank God for the power of the kingdom of God and the anointing. Through the kingdom of God the anointing destroys strongholds.

Strongholds are mental files with information about every aspect of life. If the information is negative and evil the file contains a stronghold. The stronghold must be demolished and the right information put in the file. These files are in the subconscious mind. For instance, if we want to make a money decision we must consult the money file. Thoughts are drawn from these files into the conscious mind to be considered. This is the thinking that goes on before the thinking. This means these files are carefully chosen before beginning the thought process. This is the spirit of our minds spoken about by the Bible. Ephesians 4:23 says,

"and be renewed in the spirit of your mind,"

CHAPTER 2

HOW STRONGHOLDS ARE BUILT

In chapter 1, I described strongholds as wrong thinking patterns that are contrary to the Word of God. The bricks or building blocks for strongholds are the lies of the devil. The mind is easily trained to think a particular way when it is barraged by the same truth or lie over and over again. This is how thinking patterns form. A barrage of lies or wrong concepts or conclusions about something, continually shot to the human mind, concretizes to form a formidable structure called a stronghold.

Another way to understand how strongholds are built is to analyze the ancient warfare tactic called a siege. I asked one man who was once in the military if they were still employing this method of besieging. He told me that whenever they used this method they did it with a mindset of taking over. The Merriam-Webster dictionary defines it as a military blockade of a city or fortified place to compel it to surrender. The army surrounds the city and stays there for a long time, shutting people in there until all business is brought to a halt, usually resulting in starvation. A typical example is found in 2 Kings 6:24-30. The Bible says,

"And it happened after this that Ben-Hadad king of Syria gathered all his army, and went up and besieged Samaria. And

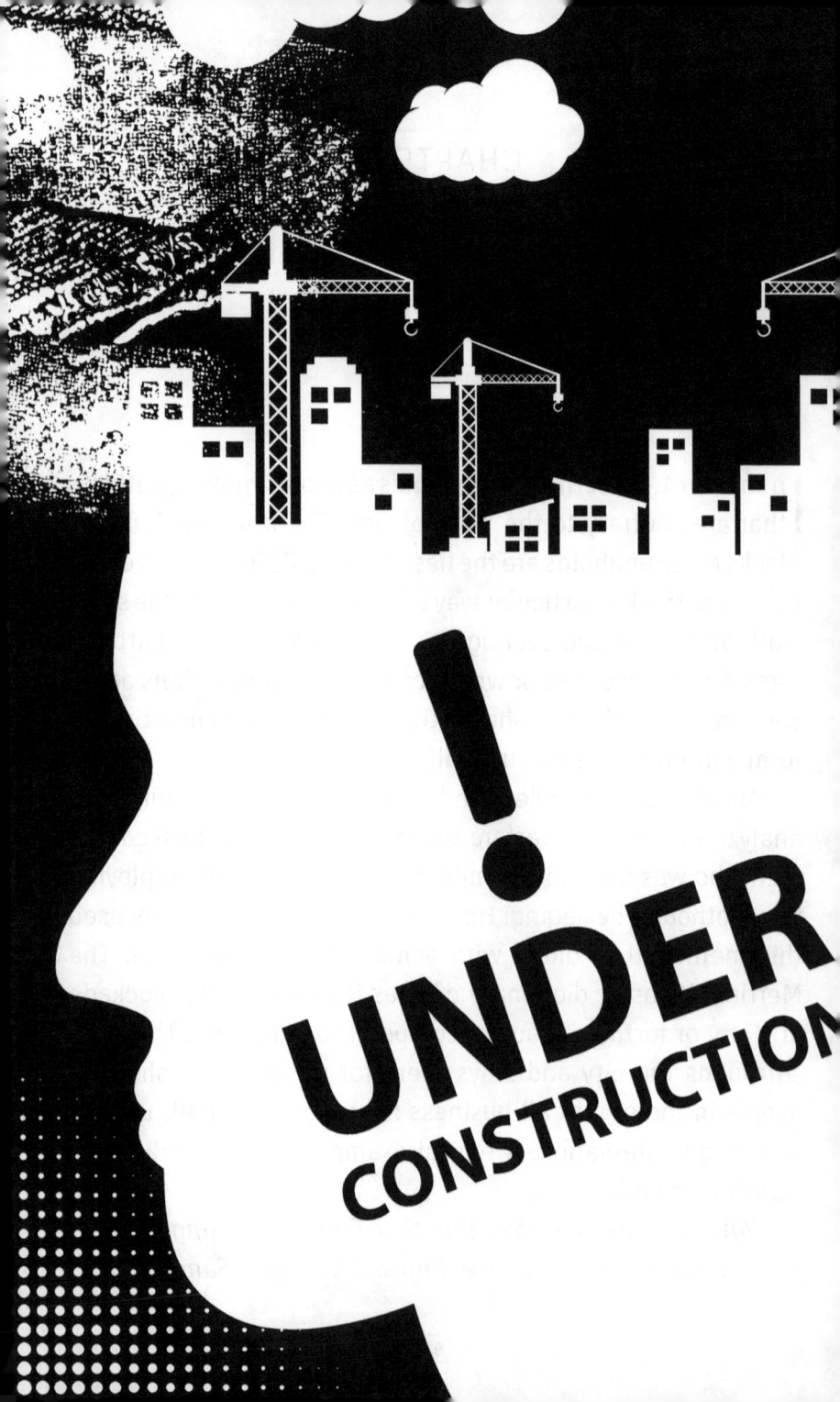

there was a great famine in Samaria; and indeed they besieged it until a donkey's head was sold for eighty shekels of silver, and one-fourth of a kab of dove droppings for five shekels of silver.

Then, as the king of Israel was passing by on the wall, a woman cried out to him, saying, "Help, my lord, O king!" And he said, "If the Lord does not help you, where can I find help for you? From the threshing floor or from the winepress?" Then the king said to her, "What is troubling you?" And she answered, "This woman said to me, 'Give your son, that we may eat him today, and we will eat my son tomorrow.' So we boiled my son, and ate him. And I said to her on the next day, 'Give your son, that we may eat him'; but she has hidden her son. Now it happened, when the king heard the words of the woman, that he tore his clothes; and as he passed by on the wall, the people looked, and there underneath he had sackcloth on his body."

The act of laying siege is called besieging. In the formation of a stronghold the army is composed of the negative, lying thoughts from the pits of hell. Those thoughts keep besieging the mind until the mind surrenders. This is why, even if the victim decides they no longer want to think that way, it is difficult to win because the mind would have surrendered. Anything that keeps coming to the mind becomes a habit (in our case a stronghold) and habits are not easy to break. Constant bombardment of the mind with a lie builds a stronghold.

The source of wrong thoughts could be ideas, concepts and philosophies you would have picked up along the journey of life – in the home you grew up, or in school, from a teacher you admired, at college or work or from hanging out with friends.

THERE ARE THREE MAJOR WAYS IN WHICH STRONGHOLDS ARE BUILT: VERBAL, MODELING AND PERSONAL EXPERIENCE

Like I mentioned briefly in my other book, "Understanding and Receiving Total Deliverance," there are three major ways in which strongholds are built: verbal, modelling and personal experience. Sometimes it is just wayward, wrong thoughts the devil shoots into the victim's mind and if this happens repeatedly a stronghold will result. At this point it is also important to note that strongholds are built based on the past, present and future. I will deal with all these concepts in the next four chapters.

I HEARD IT AND IT DID NOT AFFECT ME

CHAPTER 3

STRONGHOLDS BUILT THROUGH VERBAL ABUSE

Remember Mark 4:24 says,

"Then He said to them, "Take heed what you hear. With the same measure you use, it will be measured to you; and to you who hear, more will be given."

The Amplified version says, ". Pay attention to what you hear."

I have heard people giving counsel to others suggesting that when they hear something that will result in bad influence "it must pass through one ear and come out the other ear." This is not true. Remember there is a station between the two ears where what you hear must pass through. The station is called "the mind". Unless you learn how to combat or counter very quickly what you hear, you cannot hear it and remain the same. You can say, "I heard it and it did not affect me", but you know the truth. It really affected you. Don't ignore what you hear. If it is wrong, quickly counter it with right. It's a blessing not to hear some things or gossip.

By understanding the impact of what we hear it becomes easy to understand how things that were told us repeatedly became strongholds in our minds.

We counseled a young man who was sexually abused by a relative. When he told the ordeal to his parents the father did not believe him. The father said, "You are a liar. It's you who are gay." When we met him the young man's problem was that he had become addicted to sex with women. What the father said became a stronghold in his mind. He lived all his life trying to prove to the world that he was just a victim of sodomy but he was not gay. That's why he went about sleeping with any woman who came his way.

At this point, I think it is timely to warn parents of victims of sexual abuse to give ear to their children who come reporting such abuse and investigate the facts before taking sides and believing the abusers' side of the story. Another girl we helped was abused by a church leader and she happened to be daughter to pastors of this other church. When the girl reported this to her parents, they chose to believe their church leader and not their daughter. She moved to a far away country and a door had been opened for further abuse because she could not forgive neither the parents nor the one who had abused her. After several other sexual abuses she became addicted to sex and drugs. We taught her to forgive. She did it and all the strongholds were destroyed. Do you see how one stronghold, if not dealt with, can quickly give way to several other strongholds? In her case, the sexual abuse from a church leader was very traumatic. She carried this pain until she finally confessed the incident to her parents. The parents did not believe her story and began to verbally abuse her and defend the criminal. One devastating tragedy over another increased the level of pain that caused

WHAT IS SAID TO YOU CAN TURN INTO A STRONGHOLD THAT WILL SHAPE YOUR LIFE. IT IS EASY TO BECOME WHAT IS SAID TO AND ABOUT YOU UNLESS YOU QUICKLY RECEIVE HELP

the victim to trust no one and to suspect everyone. The actual incident and the subsequent denial and rejection was pouring concrete on an open wound. Her unresolved injustices led to the stronghold of unforgiveness which later resulted in strongholds of further abuse and addiction.

With all these real-life examples and many others we cannot write about now, it is indicative that strongholds should be dealt with without delay. It becomes critically paramount for Christian leaders to teach the church and assist in the pulling down of strongholds. Teaching is needful because many are suffering from the torment of strongholds yet not knowing what they are and let alone how to deal with them.

A man called Peter Daniels, in his book, "Miss Phillips You Were Wrong" (page 13-14), has this to say,

"But Miss Phillips thundered down between the desks towards me and slapped my face, stood me up, shook me and punched my back and then finally took the point of my chin between her forefinger and thumb and shook with all her strength yelling, 'Peter Daniels, you are a bad, bad boy and you are never going to amount to anything.'

That event both crashed and angered me and was to dog me for the rest of my school years. It affected my attitude and ability to the point where it became, in a sense, a self-fulfilling prophecy.

We all come into contact with a Mr. or Miss Phillips in life. They may have different names, they may come from different stations in life, they could even be someone close like a brother, sister, mother or father, relative, friend or stranger."

What is said to you can turn into a stronghold that will shape your life. It is easy to become what is said to and about you unless you quickly receive help. The situation is worsened by the painful truth that our arch-enemy, Satan, will quickly take advantage of the situation by assigning a demon to be housed in the stronghold from the verbal abuse to make sure what was said against the victim will come to pass and be part of his or her life.

The mind, if untrained, cannot stand against something that is repeatedly said to it over a long period. It will soon register it as truth and that supposed "truth" becomes cemented in the mind as a stronghold .

Just imagine the impact of negative words like:

"You are poor!"

"You will never amount to anything!"

"No one in your family has ever prospered!"

"You are a failure!"

"You are dumb!"

"You will always be sick!"

"You will die of heart disease like people in your family tree!"

"You will never be delivered!"

"You will never be healed!"

"You will never be married!"

"You will never have children!"

"You will be divorced like everyone else in your family!"

"You are bad!"

"You are a failure!"

The list is endless.

Some will say,

"It can't be done!"

"The opportunities are not there!"

"The timing is all wrong!"

"You don't have the ability!"

"You are not qualified!"

If any of these is said to the victim repeatedly, it easily becomes a stronghold in his or her mind and it can determine the outcome of his or her life, if not dealt with.

CHAPTER 4

STRONGHOLDS BUILT THROUGH WHAT WAS OR IS BEING MODELED

It is true that life is more caught than taught. We easily believe and become what we see being modeled before us as we grow. Up until they receive the truth about what a Christian marriage looks like, many Christians will live the married life they saw being modeled or demonstrated by their parents or guardians. Unfortunately some can follow the pattern of the marriage they saw in their favorite childhood movies or television shows. In other words the media also has a great part to play in the formation of strongholds in innocent and unsuspecting minds. Actually, in the case of the marriage example I gave, two kinds of strongholds can ensue. One can have the exact kind of marriage that was modeled and another can go to the other extreme where they strive to do the exact opposite of what they saw being modeled. I will explain this further in detail when I open the discussion on marital strongholds.

If someone's parents would always get broke and ended up borrowing every month, it becomes easy for a stronghold of debt to be built up in a young growing mind. This would be the concept of money that was modeled. The lie that is used to build up the stronghold is, "it's not bad to borrow when you

are broke and it's normal to be broke." The person who grew up in such an environment finds it easy to borrow. They borrow casually and without hesitation. Depending on whether those who modeled this lifestyle paid back their loans, the victim of this stronghold may or may not pay back what they borrowed and that without remorse. It's a learned behaviour.

Strongholds built through modeling manifest in many different forms and we cannot exhaust them in this single chapter. Sometimes the way one speaks is very indicative of what was modeled before them as they were growing up. In Spiritual Warfare 1, I called it speech perversion. A talkative behavior, say, is a great clue as to the environment one grew up in, where maybe they grew up seeing people who spoke that way.

A person who grew up in an environment where cursing was the norm can be found, today, to be a curse fountain. Words of cursing flow naturally, effortlessly and unceasingly like he or she has an internal dictionary or Thesaurus of curse words. Unless that stronghold, built from the environment of cursing he or she grew up in, is pulled down, any desire to change the way he or she speaks will be frustratingly futile. The same goes with an individual who, as he or she grew up, had hostility, verbal and physical fighting modeled before them. To him or her arguing and shouting and cursing is normal and permissible. It's a way of life and they do it with no sense of guilt or remorse. They ignorantly exhibit a behavior that is sincerely wrong but because it's a stronghold from a lifestyle that was modeled, they have no clue that that kind of behaviour is wrong.

A PERSON WHO GREW UP IN AN ENVIRONMENT WHERE CURSING WAS THE NORM CAN BE FOUND, TODAY, TO BA A CURSE FOUNTAIN. WORDS OF CURSING FLOW NATURALLY, EFFORTLESSLY AND UNCEASINGLY LIKE THEY HAVE AN INTERNAL DICTIONARY OR THESAURUS OF CURSE WORDS

I will also bring additional clarity to the formation of strongholds through modelling as I will be discussing about the related subject of strongholds built through background or past experience. A modeled life is an integral part of our background and it is difficult to differentiate the two.

Strongholds from modeled lives range from very minor bad behavioural patterns to evil ways of thinking and behavior which, like I mentioned earlier, can be harnessed by demons to make sure the strongholds are maintained, reinforced mercilessly, negatively influencing, and dominating the life of the victim.

Remember, I said strongholds are not actual demons but they can function as demonic houses. The wrong thinking pattern attracts demons that will enforce and enhance the evil outcome from these wrong and evil mental frameworks.

On the minor side, a story is told about a woman who, before she put sausages in a frying pan, cut off both ends of the sausage, making it shorter. Her daughter asked why and she responded, "I don't know. I saw my mother doing it all the time." The daughter went to her grandmother to ask and her first response was intense laughter before she said, "I had a small pan and had to make sure the sausages fit in the pan so I cut both ends. Your mother saw me do it but didn't know why." That is the power of modeling.

PAST

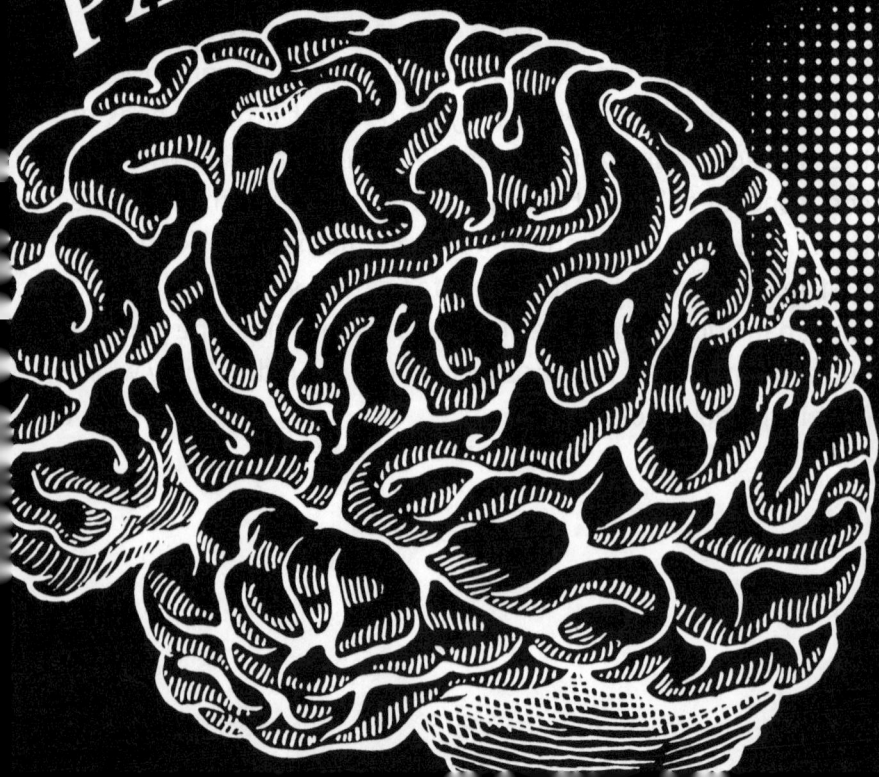

CHAPTER 5

STRONGHOLDS BUILT THROUGH BACKGROUND OR PAST EXPERIENCES

These could be experiences that happened way back in the formative stages of one's life or they could be from the near or recent past. They could also be issues that are currently being experienced. It could be a one time, one-off experience or maybe it was a repeated experience. The results are usually the same.

A young child who witnesses a traumatic event can grow up under the menacing stronghold of fear. Unless he or she exposes that root of the fear and realizes it is a stronghold that must be pulled down, all his or her efforts to overcome fear will yield no results.

A child who grows up in an abusive environment, be it verbal, sexual, emotional or physical, can end up thinking it is normal to be abused. This can open up a door to be continually abused even in adulthood. As I will explain later, an undealt with stronghold of abuse can lead into other strongholds and the victim ends up with a myriad of strongholds to be pulled down.

A story is told about a girl whose parents always had heated arguments whenever they got money. Maybe it was about who

A CHILD WHO GROWS UP IN AN ABUSIVE ENVIRONMENT, BE IT VERBAL, SEXUAL, EMOTIONAL OR PHYSICAL, CAN END UP THINKING IT IS NORMAL TO BE ABUSED. THIS CAN OPEN UP A DOOR TO BE CONTINUALLY ABUSED EVEN IN ADULTHOOD

would and how it was going to be spent. One day, while eating as a family in a restaurant, the same argument arose. The father stood up and was raving at his wife when he suddenly collapsed and died from a heart attack. It was so traumatic for the girl to be an eyewitness of such a heart-wrenching event. There was no one trained to help him. No one even attempted CPR. The reason for telling the story is the painful fact that this girl grew up not desiring to have more money than she needed. She enjoyed just breaking even. In her mind, a stronghold developed that said, "Having extra money causes arguments that may result in death." Every time she got money more than what she required to just break even, something would just happen that would expend that extra cash. It would happen without her having to think about it.

To add salt to the wound, she ended up becoming a nurse. A job she never enjoyed because it was not her passion, calling or purpose. Another stronghold made her to become a nurse because no one was available to help when her father passed. She made this decision without even remembering the event. It was a stronghold in the mind. I am sure from this story we can clearly see the role of past experiences in the construction of strongholds.

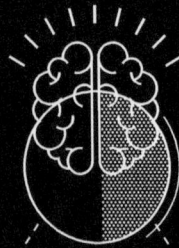

PAST

FUTURE

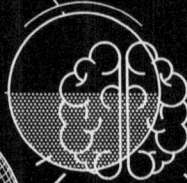

PRESENT

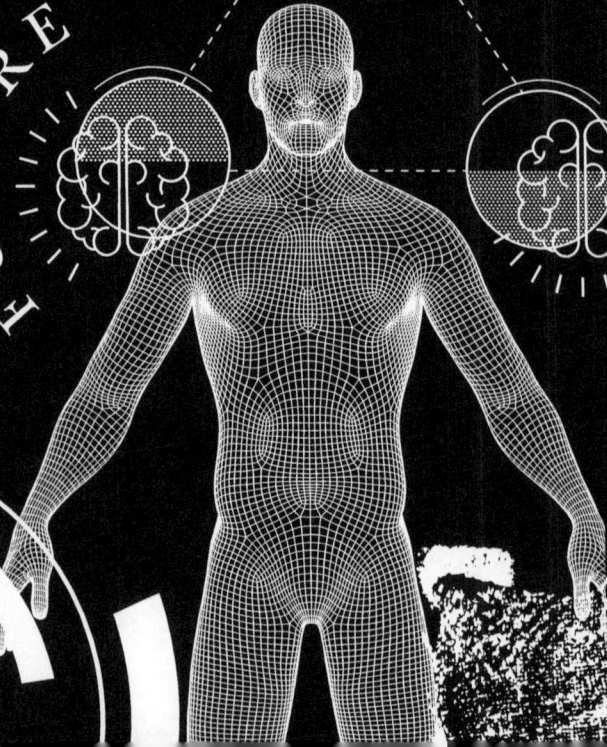

CHAPTER 6

THE PAST, PRESENT AND FUTURE TENSE OF STRONGHOLD FORMATION

Before we conclude how strongholds are formed, let us consider that the formative methods of strongholds can be easily categorized into past, present and future. It's easy to understand this from the perspective of the past since we have discussed about past experiences but we may need more elaboration on the present and the future.

Concerning the past, a lot of emotional strongholds emanate from one's past. These include anger, depression, discouragement, frustration, inferiority complex, superiority complex, fear and countless other volatile feelings.

Overcoming emotional strongholds involves going deeper than your feelings to discover the root cause behind them e.g. abused as a child, raped, betrayed in a relationship, or being unwanted. The strongholds are rooted in the past. Emotional damage happened during a person's developmental years either through trauma, neglect or any number of negative factors. These situations create emotional grooves in our minds that eventually become part of our normal mode of life.

It is not easy to forget the past when you think you are responsible for what happened. Forgive yourself and stop beating up yourself. Deal with self-condemnation and condemnation from people and from Satan. Usually people with a painful past can end up being hypocritical or bipolar. They find it difficult to live their real self. Becoming the real you can be painful because you remember all the pain you went through hence you try to be another person. Never camouflage pain. Pour it out as soon as possible.

Now let's consider the present.

Imagine a married couple who have been having communication issues for the past two weeks. The wife has concluded that her husband does not love her because of how he is communicating harshly to her. A stronghold has been built based on prevailing, present circumstances.

Maybe things are going on at your workplace and people seem like they are all against you. You also conclude, in your mind, that "people don't love me." A stronghold has been built in the face of present circumstances. Sometimes it's important to deal with issues exclusively without drawing permanent conclusions as to people's attitudes towards you. As things are happening it is important to interpret them from God's perspective. Many times we just need to forgive and move on, never allowing strongholds to be formed about those people and those events. This is why we are always taught never to make important decisions during emotional turmoil.

The future tense of stronghold formation can be easily understood by way of illustration. Usually it is caused by fear, worry or anxiety about the future. Questions like these flood and besiege one's mind:

OVERCOMING EMOTIONAL STRONGHOLDS INVOLVES GOING DEEPER THAN YOUR FEELINGS TO DISCOVER THE ROOT CAUSE BEHIND THEM E.G. ABUSED AS A CHILD, RAPED, BETRAYED IN A RELATIONSHIP, OR BEING UNWANTED

"What if I discovered I have cancer?"
"What if my son dies?"
"What if I lose all my money?"
"What if I die?"

All those can be strongholds based on the future. It usually happens when the devil suggests these negative thoughts or when something happens to someone else or somewhere or when one hears negative reports, say, from doctors.

Strongholds from fear of the future can be so tormenting and they paralyze the victim which can lead to a non-productive life. They stop planning for their future. One year my wife got ill for almost two years. The devil started attacking her with the relentless thoughts of "you're going to die!" Life started losing meaning. I tried to share future plans we could pursue as a family but already I was alone in it. I tried to draw plans of the house we intended to build but in her mind she visualized me staying in that house with another wife. It got worse until the devil caused her to begin to visualize her own funeral. That's how tormenting strongholds based on the future can be. Lies about the future can form formidable strongholds in people's minds. When she began to confess that she would not die, the stronghold lost is hold and she was healed.

One preacher told his congregation that Jesus was coming to rapture the church the following year. They believed him and a lot of them withdrew and spent all their investments and savings. Everything they were now doing depended on the delusion (stronghold) that "Jesus is coming next year." It becomes apparent that strongholds are built on lies, be they from people or from the devil.

CHAPTER 7

MOTIVATION TO PULL DOWN STRONGHOLDS

In his book, Two Ways Of Knowing God (page 51-52), Apostle Ezekiel Guti has this to say,

"When a person believes in Jesus, according to Romans 10:9-10, his spirit is completely saved. What remains is the teaching of possessing the land. The war is in the mind. . To enjoy the Kingdom of God we must fight with what is in our flesh. If you overcome anger you get the blessing. Whatever you overcome, blessing will take over. When you overcome adultery and fornication you get blessing. Salvation and eternal life we have already. But we have war in our flesh and mind. We must conquer. It does not mean such people will not go to heaven but while on earth they are hindered from receiving blessings because of what is in the flesh and mind. The battle is in the mind. The war to get the blessing is in the mind."

You cannot be stronger than your mind. When your mind is weak then you are weak. We need to know that from the day we got born again we turned our backs from and declared war on a persistent enemy. We are all soldiers in this war. Like I said, in Volume 1, there are no civilians. It's about how we are doing

THE DEVIL IS ALWAYS WATCHING

in this war and not about whether we are in a war or not. No wonder why the Bible says, in 2 Corinthians 10:4,

"For the weapons of our warfare are not carnal but mighty in God for pulling down strongholds,"

The Bible also says, in 2Timothy 2:4,

"No one engaged in warfare entangles himself with the affairs of this life, that he may please him who enlisted him as a soldier."

In 1Peter 5:8, the Bible warns us,

"Be sober, be vigilant; because your adversary the devil walks about like a roaring lion, seeking whom he may devour."

The devil is always watching for a moment when you are weak to get at you. It has been his chief goal and purpose, after his whooping , first in heaven (Revelations 12:7-12) and through the cross (Hebrews 2:14-15, Colossians 2:15), to get back to God by defeating God's children. If he can win and control your mind he can control you. That's why I firmly affirm and submit to you that you cannot be stronger than your mind.

With the kind of fierce and ruthless enemy the devil is, surely I cannot give in and give up and allow this tormenting creature to take charge of my mind. Once the devil takes charge of your mind he has taken charge of your life. I am highly motivated to demolish these strongholds. I've made up my mind. I've made a concrete decision. I've mastered all my spiritual, mental, and physical energy to demolish every stronghold. Our key text, 2 Corinthians 10:4-5, says,

"For the weapons of our warfare are not carnal but mighty in God for pulling down strongholds, casting down arguments

and every high thing that exalts itself against the knowledge of God, bringing every thought into captivity to the obedience of Christ,"

The mind is like a statehouse or presidential palace. Once an enemy attempting a coup de tat takes over the State House, they have taken over power. The same thing happens with the key television station in a country. The American electoral system is such that a candidate who wins particular states in a close or tight contest can possibly win the presidency. The devil wins once he wins over your mind. Both God and the devil win or lose you in your mind. My spiritual father, Apostle Ezekiel Guti repeats over and over again saying, "The battle is in the mind." This is why on several occasions the Bible warns us to "guard our minds." (Philippians 4:7, 1 Peter 1:13, Proverbs 4:23)

Philippians 4:7 says,

"and the peace of God, which surpasses all understanding, will guard your hearts and minds through Christ Jesus."

1 Peter 1:13 also says,

"Therefore gird up the loins of your mind, be sober, and rest your hope fully upon the grace that is to be brought to you at the revelation of Jesus Christ;"

The Word of God admonishes us in Proverbs 4:23, saying,

"Keep your heart with all diligence, For out of it spring the issues of life."

Any stronghold you won't demolish will ultimately destroy you. Through the stronghold, the devil can steal your life, one day at a time. Kevin Gerald, in his book, "Mind Monsters (page 45)", says,

"Feelings originate from thoughts, and thoughts originate in the mind. You can change the way you feel by changing the way you think."

The devil can steal away your joy, your peace, your self-esteem, your confidence, your productivity, by simply taking over your mind. By triggering a thought about how someone offended you thirty years ago, the stronghold can affect your mood and take away your peace and joy. The whole day can become unproductive and lost. Life is measured in terms of time. That's why when they ask how old you are you answer in terms of time and say, "I am twenty years old." By stealing your days the devil, who came to steal, kill and destroy, is able to kill you one day at a time.

If, for some reason known to the individual and Satan, one refuses or becomes naïve concerning pulling down strongholds, they lose grip of their eternal crown and the prize of the high calling of God. They risk longevity in serving God. The enemy causes them not to be able to fulfil their purpose in life and in the Kingdom of God. This is all possible because the stronghold is able to influence how one behaves because it produces thoughts which produce feelings and ultimately actions that are contrary to God's will.

As I am writing, the visionary in our ministry, Archbishop Ezekiel Guti, is this year emphasizing tirelessly about how we should dominate and walk in spiritual authority as Kingdom Children and Ambassadors. To wage war and dominate we all need "the mind of Christ." 1 Corinthians 2:16 says,

WITH THE KIND OF FIERCE AND RUTHLESS ENEMY THE DEVIL IS, SURELY I CANNOT GIVE IN AND GIVE UP AND ALLOW THIS TORMENTING CREATURE TO TAKE CHARGE OF MY MIND. ONCE THE DEVIL TAKES CHARGE OF YOUR MIND HE HAS TAKEN CHARGE OF YOUR LIFE

"For 'who has known the mind of the Lord that he may instruct Him?' But we have the mind of Christ."

The mind of Christ cannot manifest in us if our minds have undemolished strongholds. In essence I am submitting to you that with strongholds in your life and in your mind you cannot practice the kingdom of God because you cannot practice righteousness. You cannot rule, control and dominate as God purposes you to.

In the year that God spoke to his choice servant, prophet Ezekiel Guti, and gave the annual theme of "Walking in total deliverance", I attended a session where he said, "I cannot afford to lose the joy of seeing the power of the Kingdom of God manifested because of sin, because of not being delivered."

It is so sweet and fulfilling to walk in the power of the Kingdom of God. This is why we must all be motivated to demolish all the strongholds from our minds and from our lives.

Did you know that some strongholds can affect relationships with other people. This is because the stronghold produces thoughts and the thoughts produce feelings and the feelings cause commensurate actions. If the stronghold can cause a bad mood or bad feelings, already it affects your relationship with people around you. The stronghold can cause wrong actions which can affect your relationship with the people around you. This means strongholds can adversely affect your relationships. It can cause divorce and it can sever relationships that were once strong because it can change the way you behave. Be motivated to destroy those strongholds now. Don't postpone it. It has to be now before the enemy takes root in those strongholds. Strongholds of anger can cause you to exhibit fits of rage which can cause you to do things that can end you in prison, all because the stronghold of anger was not pulled down.

Why wait until you are facing a divorce? Why wait until you encounter a huge financial crisis? Why wait until you do something in a fit of anger that lands you in a prison cell? Why not begin today to pull down all those strongholds and to retrain the mind?

I know people who will say, "You don't understand my life. You don't understand what happened to me." Sometimes people use their circumstances to excuse their negative mindset. They justify living in worry, intimidation and fear. It's time to confront it now. It's time to pull down every stronghold.

In later chapters I am going to expose some of the most tormenting, destructive and life-threatening strongholds. Of course I will also touch on the seemingly small, minor ones though I don't consider them minor because they have a huge potential to grow. For each stronghold I will discuss what it is, it's nature, how it is formed and how it can be demolished or the truth that demolishes it.

CHAPTER 8

HOW TO PULL DOWN STRONGHOLDS

2 Corinthians 10:4-5 says,

"For the weapons of our warfare are not carnal but mighty in God for pulling down strongholds, casting down arguments and every high thing that exalts itself against the knowledge of God, bringing every thought into captivity to the obedience of Christ,"

The New International Version says,

"The weapons we fight with are not the weapons of the world. On the contrary, they have divine power to demolish strongholds. We demolish arguments and every pretension that sets itself up against the knowledge of God, and we take captive every thought to make it obedient to Christ."

The bible says, "...that exalts itself against the knowledge of God." It's important to always remind our minds that nothing is bigger or more powerful than God. Nothing is more powerful than Jesus. Absolutely nothing! Not even the strongest addiction. We need to downsize everything that comes against us relative to the greatness of our God and our Lord Jesus Christ.

WE NEED TO TELL OUR MINDS THAT NOTHING IS BIGGER OR MORE POWERFUL THAN GOD

Our warfare is to get back our thought lives and instead take them and make them captive to the obedience of Christ.

We have discussed that strongholds are formed through constant bombardment of the victim's mind with a lie or lies. We said the mind is besieged with lies and negativity. In the same vein, strongholds are pulled down by constant bombardment of the mind with Truth. Once again we have to besiege the mind, but this time with Truth. Truth from the Word of God.

The Greek word for demolish is "katairesis". It comes from two Greek words: 'kata' which means opposed to, against, contrary to and 'haireomai' which means to choose. Therefore the meaning of the word demolish is to choose something that is contrary to, against or opposed to. To demolish strongholds, we must therefore choose truth that is against or contrary to the lie that built the stronghold. We don't need a better course of action, not to do right – but to choose truth. Human effort would not do the job. Strongholds, like their name, are too strong for human effort to prevail. We need to choose Truth in order to pull down strongholds and nothing else.

Have you ever noticed that when we rely on human effort to deal with strongholds we always end up frustrated and despondent. How many times have we made New Year's resolutions to deal with certain strongholds but to no avail. Some of us get stronger every time we fail as we proclaim, "God, I will never do it again." After a few days or even hours, we get weak and do it again and we declare, "Forgive me Lord, I will never do it again." Such issues are common among the addicted. We actually hate the behaviour with a passion and

THE PROBLEM IS THAT WE ASSUME THAT OUR BEHAVIOR IS THE BATTLEFIELD AND MAKE CHANGING OUR ACTIONS THE GOAL INSTEAD OF CHANGING OUR INITIAL THOUGHTS. THE MOST EFFECTIVE WAY TO INFLUENCE BEHAVIOR IS TO INFLUENCE THE THINKING

then we do it again. It's really frustrating and we can feel helpless and useless. The problem is that we assume that our behaviour is the battlefield and make changing our actions the goal instead of changing our initial thoughts. The most effective way to influence behaviour is to influence the thinking.

It becomes a frustrating, vicious cycle when we rely solely on human effort. WE JUST NEED TRUTH!! It's so true, like my spiritual father, Prophet Ezekiel Guti says, that the anointing pulls down strongholds. The anointing has to do with the working of the Holy Spirit and He works using the Truth of the Word of God we have believed. The anointing without the Truth will not do the job. If it does, it will be very temporary. Choose Truth! Choose Truth! Choose Truth! Hunt for it! Hunt for Truth that counters the lie that built the stronghold. If it was a painful experience seek for truth that fosters inner healing and forgiveness. Didn't Jesus say,

"you shall know the truth and the truth will make you free." (John 8:32)

The truth that sets you free is not only the truth you know but the truth you are intimate with (the Hebrew concept of 'knowing' as found in Genesis 4:1) and believe in. You have to believe it is true for you and that you are receiving what it says. Then keep bombarding your mind with the same truth, sometimes from different Scriptures. Let the Truth of God be the dominant thought patterns governing your life.

Seek Truth as you listen to the teaching of the Word of God concerning the area in which you intend to pull down the stronghold or strongholds. Seek Truth as you read and study God's Word and other good sources of truth that agrees with God's Word.

At this time, it is paramount that I highlight to you that we have to go deeper than just bombarding the mind with Truth. We have to retrain the mind to think right – to be healed and delivered from the wrong pattern of thinking that had been going on for so long. It's retraining as well as guarding against further attack. In other words, now we must build a positive stronghold, with Truth this time around.

The process to pull down strongholds involves Recognizing them, Rejecting them, Replacing them and Retraining the mind. It must be easy to remember "the four R's". We will analyse this process in the following chapters.

CHAPTER 9

RECOGNIZING STRONGHOLDS

The first, very important, step in curing a disease is its diagnosis. It is important, before answering a question, to know and understand the question. You cannot solve a problem you don't know. You cannot pull down a stronghold without first seeing that you have one and you need to pull it down.

One of the easiest ways to know that there is a stronghold in your mind is when you notice that you have persistent wayward thoughts. One good example is wayward sexual thoughts which just come and you feel you cannot control them. Right there is another stronghold. The devil tells you that you can't control your thoughts. If you agree to his suggestion you will be tormented and frustrated by these thoughts for a long time. The truth is that your mind can be retrained to think right. As long as you are not insane you are in charge of your mind even if there could be demonic influence or presence in your life. The battle is in the mind. Strongholds are not an excuse for the choices we make in our minds. I know demons can influence our thinking and our decisions but we have the final say. One man fell into adultery and said afterwards, "I don't know what happened. I found myself in it. We fight the iniquity of adultery in our family tree. It's spiritual, really demonic."

DIAGNOSIS

The truth is that those kinds of spirits exist and they can influence victims but the final say is always in the victim's mind unless he or she is insane. The demon has no hands to remove your pants. You decide to do it. You have the potential to say no to any kind of influence. People should not deny responsibility for their actions, laying all blame on iniquity or strongholds.

Do you know that people can still commit adultery with or without the influence of demons. This is because we have inherited the sinful nature just by being Adam's posterity. The "works of the flesh" are characteristics we have inherited from Adam. (Romans 5:12-21, Galatians 5:19-21)

To recognize strongholds one also needs to pay attention to internal dialogue. The guy who buried the talent he received had internal dialogue. He said, in Matthew 25:24-25,

"Then he who had received the one talent came and said, 'Lord, I knew you to be a hard man, reaping where you have not sown, and gathering where you have not scattered seed. And I was afraid, and went and hid your talent in the ground. Look, there you have what is yours.'"

To the one who was given the least, an internal dialogue was dominating his actions. He hid what little he had and adopted a negative attitude toward the One who gave it to him. He thought he was right but he was wrong. His wrong thinking forced him to forfeit his wealth and worse still, his relationship with his supplier.

The woman who had an issue of blood had a positive internal dialogue. She said, in Mark 5:28,

"For she said, "If only I may touch His clothes, I shall be made well."

Who was she talking to? It was an internal dialogue.

The prodigal son had a serious internal dialogue. In Luke 15:17-20, the Bible says,

"But when he came to himself, he said, 'How many of my father's hired servants have bread enough and to spare, and I perish with hunger! I will arise and go to my father, and will say to him, "Father, I have sinned against heaven and before you, and I am no longer worthy to be called your son. Make me like one of your hired servants."' And he arose and came to his father. But when he was still a great way off, his father saw him and had compassion, and ran and fell on his neck and kissed him."

The mind is made up of two main parts: the conscious mind and the subconscious mind. The subconscious mind is the storage unit and the conscious mind is the processing unit. There are files or folders in the subconscious mind that relate to every discipline of life. When one is making a financial decision, say, they have to refer to the money file that is in the subconscious mind. If the file has wrong information it is a stronghold. Different thoughts have to leave the subconscious mind to be processed in the conscious mind. It is during this movement that the internal dialogue takes place. This is the process we sometimes refer to as reasoning. When we say we are exercising self-control, we are referring to the internal dialogue. We have to take charge of the internal dialogue and win. This is why Apostle Ezekiel Guti always says,

ONE OF THE EASIEST WAYS TO KNOW THAT THERE IS A STRONGHOLD IN YOUR MIND IS WHEN YOU NOTICE THAT YOU HAVE PERSISTENT WAYWARD THOUGHTS

"Don't allow your mind to think what it wants." Sometimes I preach to my own mind and ask questions like, "Do you have a Scripture for what you want me to think?" There is power in mastering the internal dialogue.

The fact is, many times in a day, internal dialogue is always taking place in an individual's life. Listening to these dialogues and measuring them against the standard of God's Word can provide a clue to whether strongholds exist in a person's life or not. Make the Holy Spirit the referee or the umpire of your internal dialogue.

One must always pay attention to moods. The way one feels at any given time springs from their thoughts. You can change the way you feel by changing the way you think. One can become moody without anyone having to offend them. It can happen by just thinking. Remember we said the strongholds produce thoughts and thoughts produce feelings and feelings produce actions. Sometimes the thoughts are about what happened in the past but sometimes the victim just imagines things that never happened or may never happen and those thoughts can insidiously cause mood swings in the victim.

Attention must also be paid to our conversations. How one speaks, especially when it's persistent and consistent, can be a very apparent indicator of the presence of a stronghold. If, in conversations, an individual always alludes or directly refers to their inability to do things because they are poor, this can be indicative of a stronghold of poverty. If someone's conversations are always negative, it is a clear sign that there is a stronghold to pull down. The Bible says, in Luke 6:45,

"A good man out of the good treasure of his heart brings forth good; and an evil man out of the evil treasure of his heart brings forth evil. For out of the abundance of the heart his mouth speaks."

To recognize strongholds, we have to recognize thoughts that are inconsistent with God's thoughts. God's thoughts can be found nowhere else except in His Word.

STOP FEEDING IT

CHAPTER 10

STOP FEEDING THAT STRONGHOLD!!

The first thing to do after recognizing the presence of the stronghold is to stop feeding it. As long as you are feeding a stronghold, you cannot destroy it.

Consider the stronghold of sexual perversion which we will deal with in more detail later. When one is garnering truth to demolish it and at the same time watching X-rated movies they will not be able to demolish that stronghold. I know it is the anointing, using the Truth of God's Word, that gets the job done BUT there are actions that help fortify the stronghold which we MUST deliberately and intentionally STOP or avoid.

One cannot win over the homosexual stronghold while continuing to attend that gay club. The Word of God, in 1 Peter 5:8 says,

"Be sober, be vigilant; because your adversary the devil walks about like a roaring lion, seeking whom he may devour."

As we apply "the weapons of our warfare", we need to learn to couple them with the ability to starve the stronghold. The stronghold is a living organism. If we cut its supply of nourishment it will die. Go to your audio, video and book libraries and quickly and permanently do away with all material that nourishes the stronghold you intend to demolish.

During long haul flights I used to spend those long hours, if I was awake, watching movies. Unfortunately the temptation was that the most "interesting" ones were rated R. Like many others, I used to swallow everything. My goal is to destroy and prevent any form of sexual perversion, therefore I must choose films that have no sexual content since the devil insists on perverting the mind with cinematic imagery, I have chosen to occupy thoughts in a more productive, Christlike manner.

Long haul flights have become a great, undisturbed opportunity to write books. Actually, right now, as I write, I am on a 15 hour flight. If I am not reading, writing or praying, during my flights, I watch TED talks or any other personal development- oriented shows from the TV section on the menu and all that effort is to STARVE any existing or emerging stronghold. We all have to be intentional about it.

I took time for me to join social media like Facebook. The truth is that for a long time I actually preached against it, seeing how the devil was harnessing it to destroy unsuspecting victims' marital and other relationships. How other people's characters were being shaped by social media and how it had become addictive to many was disturbing. Media tools, on their own, are neutral in character. They take upon them the character of the ones using them. When I subscribed to Facebook, or rather when my wife opened the account for me, to be more accurate, it was primarily for business purposes – mainly to advertise. It could be used positively after all, however, it must be noted that, depending on one's network of friends, one can just be a click away from profanity. It takes great discipline for

IF YOUR STRONGHOLD WAS GOSSIP OR SLANDER, STARVING IT WOULD BE DOING AWAY WITH YOUR "GOSSIP MATES" WHILE AT THE SAME TIME APPLYING THE TRUTH OF THE WORD TO DEMOLISH THAT SLANDEROUS STRONGHOLD

one to remain positive on Facebook, especially considering its addictive nature. It can be a "very reliable" source for nourishing existing or yet-to-be major strongholds. Actually social media addictions are strongholds.

The emphasis is to STARVE THAT FORTRESS !! Starve that stronghold! In fact the besieging we discussed, under How To Pull Down Strongholds, has to do with starving the city. The city was shut in until they were starving, weak and easy to destroy. This is how easy it can be for us to demolish strongholds if we learn how to starve them.

If your stronghold was gossip or slander, starving it would be doing away with your "gossip mates" while at the same time applying the Truth of the Word to demolish that slanderous stronghold.

STARVE THAT STRONGHOLD!! STOP FEEDING IT!!

CHAPTER 11

REJECTING THOUGHTS FROM THE STRONGHOLD

Once a stronghold is built in an individual, its main function is to shoot a persistent, consistent, never-ceasing barrage of wrong, tormentous and evil thoughts, into the thinking process of the victim. In order to destroy strongholds the victim must be taught how to reject those thoughts. If they don't reject those thoughts, that would spell victory to the stronghold and to the enemy.

Never give mental assent to the thoughts or lies of the devil. If someone calls you a failure, your first instinct must be to reject that lie. God has the final say. There is a need to reject inaccurate images of you. Don't internalize someone else's inaccurate and negative image of yourself. Don't accept every thought people hold about you or the image they tried to project on you.

If wrong thoughts are entertained and not rejected, they can steal one's joy and peace. They can disrupt relationships and take away one's contentment. It is impossible to live a positive life with a negative mind. Your life will be defined by the thoughts you accept or reject. Your life will turn out very differently depending on the thoughts you accept or reject.

What you allow into your mind will affect the outcome of your life.

Reject every thought that does not meet the Philippians 4:8 standard. I call it the P4:8 standard. Philippians 4:8 says,

"Finally, brethren, whatever things are true, whatever things are noble, whatever things are just, whatever things are pure, whatever things are lovely, whatever things are of good report, if there is any virtue and if there is anything praiseworthy— meditate on these things."

The Living Bible Translation says it this way,

"And now, brothers, as I close this letter, let me say this one more thing: Fix your thoughts on what is true and good and right. Think about things that are pure and lovely, and dwell on the fine, good things in others. Think about all you can praise God for and be glad about."

Do not give mental energy to a thought unless it passes the Philippians 4:8 standard.

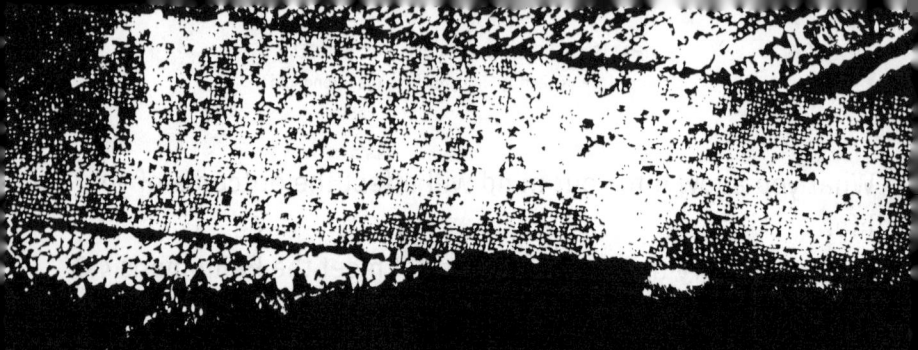

WHEN A NEGATIVE THOUGHT PULLS OUT A POSITIVE THOUGHT MUST QUICKLY REPLACE IT

CHAPTER 12

REPLACING THE WRONG THOUGHTS COMING FROM THE STRONGHOLD

It's not enough to just reject the wrong thoughts but those thoughts must be replaced by the right thoughts that measure up with God's thoughts, thoughts that line up with God's Word. Remember, God's Word is the straight edge or ruler that reveals how crooked our thoughts can be.

Have you ever been to a busy shopping mall on Christmas Eve or on Black Friday, when everyone is coming to shop at bargain prices? The parking lot will be fully packed. Sometimes you have to go round and round until someone pulls out. Our minds are like the parking lot. When a negative thought pulls out a positive thought must quickly replace it. Negative thoughts can keep going round and round and will occupy the first available space they can find.

You have to delete unimportant, wrong thoughts like you would unwanted emails but then they must be quickly replaced by good thoughts. Replace the wrong thoughts with new ones. Replace the old ways of thinking with a higher way of thinking. This is the whole jist of the sermon on the Mount. Jesus said, in Matthew 5:21-22, for example,

"You have heard that it was said to those of old, 'You shall not murder, and whoever murders will be in danger of the

THINK GOOD, FAITH-BASED THOUGHTS, FOCUSSING ON THE POSITIVE, AFFIRMING ONESELF, IMAGINING GOD DOING SOMETHING GOOD ON MY BEHALF, HOPING FOR THE BEST

judgment.' But I say to you that whoever is angry with his brother without a cause shall be in danger of the judgment. " (italics mine)

Jesus was introducing a new way of thinking.

You need to fill your mind with Philippians 4:8 thoughts. Fill your mind with thoughts that meet that standard. Ask yourself, "Am I full of true, noble, right, pure, lovely, admirable, excellent and praise-worthy thoughts?"

A businessman, W. Clement Stone, once said, "Keep your mind off the things you don't want by keeping it on the things you do want."

Think good, faith-based thoughts, focusing on the positive, affirming oneself, imagining God doing something good on my behalf, hoping for the best. Then there will be no space for worry, evil imaginations, fear, discouragement, insecurity, inferiority etc.

Don't give space to, "I wonder if they like me or not? What do they think of me?" When you reject the wrong, negative, evil thoughts quickly replace them with the good, word-based thoughts. This takes discipline. We live in a negative world. Some people are habitually programmed to think negatively about themselves. Their whole life is sum total of one low after another. They have become so accustomed to darkness and oppression that light and joy and peace are all foreign to them. But anyone can enjoy life if they "out their mind to it."

Fill the empty spots of your parking lot (your mind) by memorizing Scriptures, listening to the right Word or music, reading good books that drive home Godly principles. We must stop feeding the stronghold by depriving our minds of activities that generate the same evil thoughts that built the stronghold in the first place.

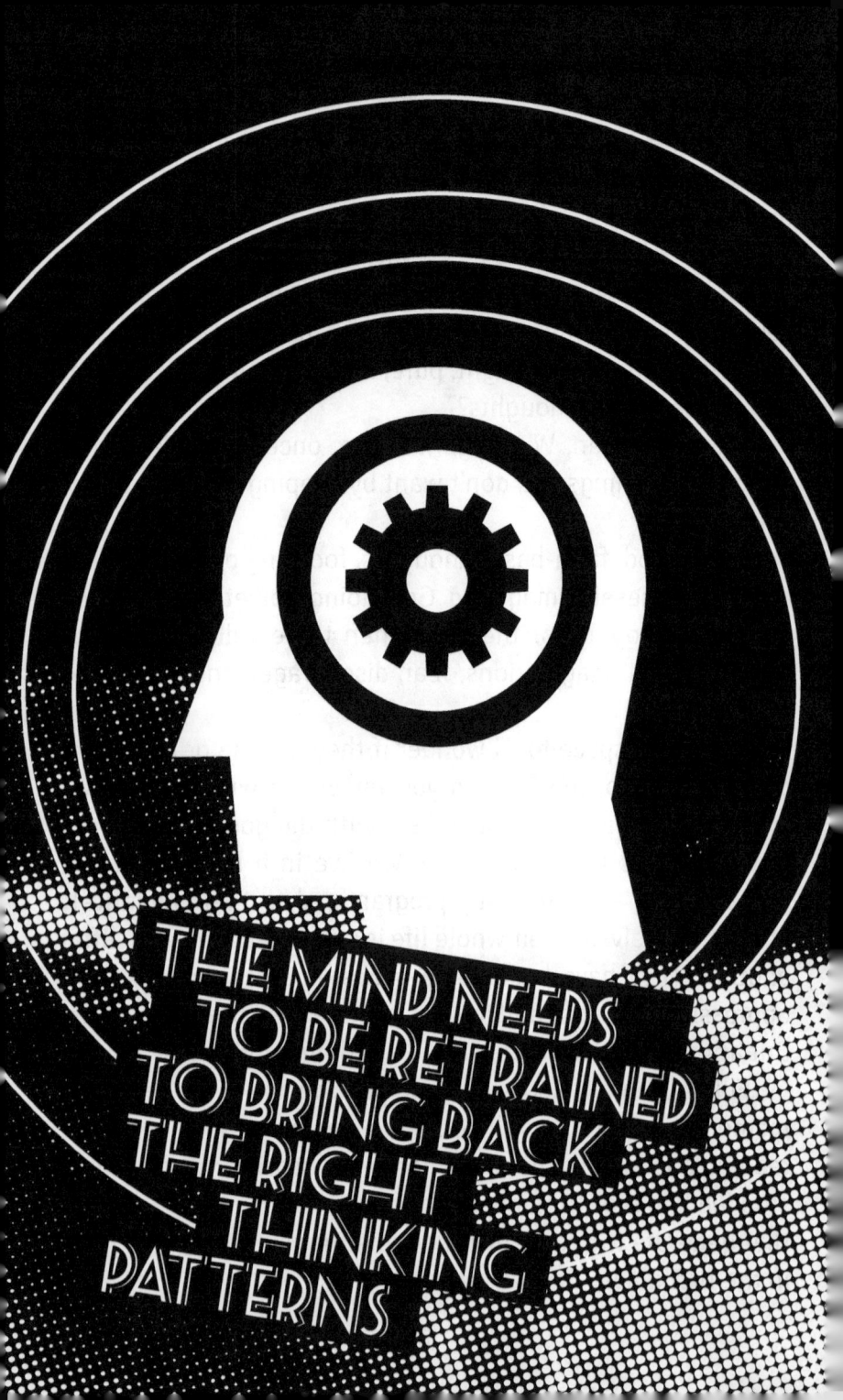

THE MIND NEEDS TO BE RETRAINED TO BRING BACK THE RIGHT THINKING PATTERNS

CHAPTER 13

RETRAINING THE MIND

To completely and permanently pull down or demolish a stronghold, the mind needs to be retrained to bring back the right thinking patterns. When specific thoughts are reinforced over a long period the mind adjusts and forms thinking habits which line up with the thoughts which are being introduced to the conscious mind. The mind is a creature of habit.

When I was at our mission house in the Cayman Islands, the water faucet (tap) would continue bringing out drops of water unless you closed it a certain way. You really had to check if water had stopped or else the water bill would be unbearable. When I returned home, to Atlanta, Georgia, it took me weeks to realize that once I shut the faucet the water would stop. I would try to shut the faucet in the style I did while in the Cayman Islands mission house. I was now in Atlanta but my mind was still in the Cayman Islands mission house kitchen. Isn't it amazing how the mind can be retrained to form a new habit?

I used to have a stronghold of the fear of turbulence during flight. However, because I enjoy reading about the flight school, I read a lot about how the plane deals with turbulence, especially the modern planes. When there is downward movement due to turbulence the plane will adjust itself to its original height without the pilot doing anything about it. No cloud nor storm can be strong enough to destroy or affect the body of the plane. Actually, one aircraft engineer told me that they test the wings by curving them until they are one meter apart. That's how strong they are. The plane has been designed to withstand extreme forces. Most planes now have systems that detect the weather ahead and they appear on different warning lights on the dashboard: green, amber and red. If it's showing red, the pilot has to divert the plane. On amber he proceeds with caution and on green he goes through normally. Lightning used to cause crashes but now they are installing lightning arrestors on planes. As I kept feeding my mind with all this information my mind got retrained. I am no longer terrified during turbulence as I fly. The mind can be retrained after all. I replaced my fear with knowledge. I gave my fear an education and it left the classroom.

Do you know that after using a road for a long time you end up driving along the road without putting your mind to it. Constant use of the road retrained your mind. You remember where lights are, where humps are and where potholes are, without thinking about it.

Once a stronghold has been pulled down there is a great need to retrain the mind never to give way again to the lies that built the stronghold in the first place. Show or give your mind what to do, what to think and it will automatically begin to form a habit. Your mind automatically thinks in habitual patterns. Your mind is a creature of habit. The mind can be trained by continuously repeating the process of recognizing, rejecting,

ONCE A STRONGHOLD HAS BEEN
PULLED DOWN THERE IS A
GREAT NEED TO RETRAIN THE
MIND NEVER TO GIVE WAY
AGAIN TO THE LIES THAT
BUILT THE STRONGHOLD
IN THE FIRST PLACE

and replacing wrong thoughts. Don't expect different results in one day or two. Some psychologists say it takes a minimum of 11 days, others say at least 21, to create a new habit. Kevin Gerald says, in his book, Mind Monsters, page 87,

"Benjamin Franklin, a great hero and leader in our nation, understood this principle. As a young man he wrote down thirteen virtues he wanted to exemplify. He focussed on one virtue each week, with the goal of absorbing that virtue into his behaviour. In thirteen weeks' time he cycled through all the virtues on his piece of paper. He repeated this sequence four times each year."

Benjamin Franklin wrote down the virtues that proclaimed, "This is the kind of man I want to be." He understood that to become a better person, he must lead his mind down a new trail of habitual thought. Show your mind where you want to go and you retrain it because it will begin to think thoughts that can lead you there.

They say, "Thoughts are like a train. They take you somewhere." Actually, strongholds are effective because they are in the mind. Where the mind goes, the life goes. Proverbs 23:7 says,

"...as he thinks in his heart so is he."

Because of this, it is common sense to conclude that unless the mind is retrained to go where we want our lives to go, we cannot overcome and demolish strongholds. The strongholds instead will determine where our lives will go.

The process of retraining the mind is the renewal of the mind that is mentioned in Romans 12:2 where the Bible says,

"And do not be conformed to this world, but be transformed by the renewing of your mind, that you may prove what is that good and acceptable and perfect will of God."

Sometimes retraining the mind involves retraining it to see God at work even in the not-so-good things. You need to tell your mind who you want to be and your mind will focus on that and it will take you there. Remember, what you focus on becomes bigger. When people watch you, they notice your habits and then describe you that way. How do you want to be described? Who do you really want to be? Tell your mind that and you become that as you train your mind to focus on that. Direct your mind towards what kind of person you want to be – decide and declare it.

Retraining the mind involves "unlearning" the wrong information from our minds and replacing it with the right information. It is replacing the wrong, evil thinking pattern with the right thinking pattern. Unless the mind is retrained stronghold formation will always recur.

YOU CONTROL.
THE MIND YOU
CONTROL THE MAN

CHAPTER 14

GUARDING THE MIND

Recently I have been listening to several prospective American Presidents as they trot the great country in their hot campaigns for presidency. Several of them are proposing the intensification of border control. This includes more border patrol and even suggestion of the construction of a wall along the Mexican border with the U.S.A. Governments, worldwide, expend billions of dollars, annually, to secure their borders.

The mind is the gateway into a man's life. Both God and the devil are in a contest for the control of that mind because once you control the mind you control the man.

We therefore, more than the governments, need to fund our minds' border control. The borders of our minds must be adequately and effectively patrolled to curb and avoid entrance by illegal thoughts.

Just like failure to come up with a reliable plan to secure the U.S.A borders may lose someone an election, failure to come up with a plan to secure the borders of our minds will cause us to lose the battle depicted in 2 Corinthians 10:4-5.

We enforce our border patrol by enforcing Philippians 4:8. This will screen all the illegal immigrants trying to gain entry into our minds. We need to plant landmines of Scripture that

THE MIND IS THE GATEWAY INTO A MAN'S LIFE. BOTH GOD AND THE DEVIL ARE IN A CONTEST FOR THE CONTROL OF THAT MIND, BECAUSE ONCE YOU CONTROL THE MIND YOU CONTROL THE MAN

will detonate every time an evil thought appears. We must guard our minds. We must guard our thought life. The Bible says to "gird the loins of our minds." (1 Peter 1:13)The Bible also says we must be "renewed in the spirit of our minds." (Ephesians 4:23)The spirit of our minds has to do with thinking that goes on before the thinking. This refers to the movement of thoughts and the internal dialogue that occurs in the subconscious mind.

Apostle Ezekiel Guti used to say,

"Don't allow your mind to think what it wants."

For years I couldn't understand what he meant. You disallow your mind to think what it wants in the "spirit of your mind." You have to give your mind what to think. This is how we guard our minds.

CHAPTER 15

THE WORK OF THE HOLY GHOST IN PULLING DOWN STRONGHOLDS

Every year in our church, God speaks to His choice servant, one of the greatest apostles of our time, Ezekiel Guti, giving him the theme of that year. This is the string or the chord we will play for the whole year. Most teachings will be centred around that theme. In 2016 the theme is "Through the Kingdom of God the anointing will pull down the strongholds." The theme text is Acts 10:38. Here the Bible says,

"how God anointed Jesus of Nazareth with the Holy Spirit and with power, who went about doing good and healing all who were oppressed by the devil, for God was with Him."

We cannot pull down any stronghold without the power and the anointing of the Holy Ghost. We cannot separate the weapon of the Word and the weapon of the Holy Ghost in our endeavour to pull down strongholds. The Bible says, in 2 Corinthians 10:4,

"For the weapons of our warfare are not carnal but mighty in God for pulling down strongholds,"

I tried to emphasize extensively that strongholds are pulled down by the Truth of the Word of God since they are built on the lies of the devil. This is so true. The enforcement and application of the Truth requires the anointing of the Holy Ghost. Just like how we say we are sanctified by the Word of God and the Holy Spirit is the agent of the process. The Holy Spirit is the power that enforces the Word of God in the pulling down of strongholds. Imagine that the Holy Ghost is like a nurse who must inject medication into a patient. The medicine is powerful but it lies dormant and ineffective if no nurse injects it into the patient. The Word of God is powerful to pull down strongholds. Hebrews 4:12 says,

"For the word of God is living and powerful, and sharper than any two-edged sword, piercing even to the division of soul and spirit, and of joints and marrow, and is a discerner of the thoughts and intents of the heart."

The Holy Ghost must inject the Truth of the Word into the core fabric of the stronghold, thereby destroying the yoke of bondage. (Isaiah 10:27)

When the stronghold is a stubborn one and the devil is whispering that you can never overcome it, that is an opportunity to have faith in the anointing of the Holy Ghost to demolish that stronghold. Remember Romans 8:11 says,

"But if the Spirit of Him who raised Jesus from the dead dwells in you, He who raised Christ from the dead will also give life to your mortal bodies through His Spirit who dwells in you."

Thank God for the Holy Ghost. No stronghold can resist "the power that raised Jesus from the dead." Our main text says, "mighty through God". Through God the Holy Spirit. The functions of the three members of the Godhead are so distinct. There is top class organization in the Trinity. Usually the Father commands. He says it. The Son does what is commanded and

WE CANNOT PULL DOWN ANY STRONGHOLD WITHOUT THE POWER AND ANOINTING OF THE HOLY GHOST. WE CANNOT SEPARATE THE WEAPON OF THE WORD OF GOD AND THE WEAPON OF THE HOLY GHOST IN OUR ENDEAVOR TO PULL DOWN STRONGHOLDS

the Holy Ghost is responsible for the power that gets it done. This actually explains why Jesus needed the Jordan River experience, when the Holy Ghost came upon Him like a dove. So we need the Holy Ghost to destroy the strongholds but He has to use the Truth of the Word of God. It is our responsibility to expose ourselves to the Word of God on a regular/daily basis. He won't do it for us but He will cooperate with us.

CHAPTER 16

THE BIG THREE

These strongholds are not big in the sense of size but in the priority we should give them in our effort to demolish strongholds. Without dealing with them first it could be really difficult to handle the other strongholds.

1. The Liberal Gospel

Sometimes I call it "the gospel of cheap grace". This is the gospel that renames sin as a weakness. Paul speaks, in Hebrew 10:26-27, and says,

"For if we sin willfully after we have received the knowledge of the truth, there no longer remains a sacrifice for sins, 27 but a certain fearful expectation of judgment, and fiery indignation which will devour the adversaries."

Sometimes a stronghold can cause people to commit, as Hebrews 12:1 says, "the sin which so easily ensnares us " The Bible says,

"Therefore we also, since we are surrounded by so great a cloud of witnesses, let us lay aside every weight, and the sin which so easily ensnares us, and let us run with endurance the race that is set before us,"

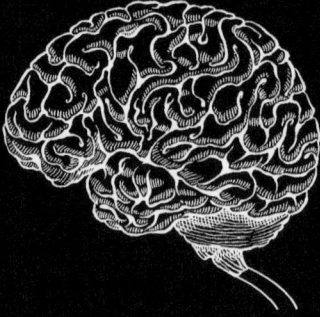

That sin or those sins expose us to the danger of impending judgment. The liberal approach will lessen the potential impact of sin on one's eternal destiny and this does damage to one's desire to demolish or deal with strongholds that are root to those sins. Today the LGBT (Lesbian- Gay-Bisexual-Transgender) movement is a big one. It's good to know that that stronghold causes a certain sinful behaviour. "Cheap grace" assumes there is no or little harm from that kind of behaviour and that kind of tolerance saps away all the energy in the victim to effectively destroy that stronghold. The liberal gospel removes the fear of judgment from perspective and victims of strongholds causing particular sins to lose motivation to deal with those strongholds.

2. Pride

The second stronghold among the "big three" is the stronghold of pride. With this stronghold in place a victim can defend or protect every other evil stronghold. Many times when proud people say, "I will not change. This is what I believe," they are actually defending that stronghold. The stronghold of pride says, "I know it all. I can do everything. I don't need help. I have it all together."

The main challenge in dealing with strongholds is that the victim rarely knows that they possess that stronghold unless they receive a revelation when it is being taught or unless someone else tells them. When a victim of the stronghold of pride is told that they have a certain stronghold they will not accept or receive it. Now, we can see why pride is one of the first "big three strongholds" to be demolished before any other. Usually the proud person "has no issues." They are perfect and seldom wrong. A proud person needs no correction or rebuke let alone to be told that they have a stronghold. What an insult! Such people have "a holier than thou" attitude and they can go to the grave with "their" strongholds. The worst or most terrible work of the stronghold of pride is its propensity to deny the existence of a stronghold or strongholds in one's life. James 4:10 says,

"Humble yourselves in the sight of the Lord, and He will lift you up."

Proverbs 16:18 also says,

"Pride goes before destruction, and a haughty spirit before a fall."

3. Unbelief

The third of the "big three" strongholds is the stronghold of unbelief. Once the devil succeeds in constructing a stronghold of unbelief or doubt in your mind, you become paralyzed to deal with every other stronghold. Have you ever had thoughts like, "You cannot overcome this stronghold. Accept it as part of your life," "You have tried so many times but you are still stuck with this stronghold," "It's normal to think that way," "Everyone else is doing it so why do you want to change?" or "You will not go to hell for this."

Once this doubt sets in it incapacitates the victim to demolish even the less tenacious stronghold. There is a need to believe God's Word instead. One needs to know that we are the temple of God and God is willing to help and empower us to demolish every stronghold. Isaiah 10:27 says,

"It shall come to pass in that day that his burden will be taken away from your shoulder, and his yoke from your neck, and the yoke will be destroyed because of the anointing oil."

In Acts 10:38, the Bible says,

"how God anointed Jesus of Nazareth with the Holy Spirit and with power, who went about doing good and healing all who were oppressed by the devil, for God was with Him."

Again the Bible says, in Numbers 13:30,

"Then Caleb quieted the people before Moses, and said, "Let us go up at once and take possession, for we are well able to overcome it.""

It's a lie from the pits of hell that you cannot overcome that addiction. The Bible says, in Philippians 4:13,

"I can do all things through Christ who strengthens me."

Paul says, in Ephesians 3:20,

"Now to Him who is able to do exceedingly abundantly above all that we ask or think, according to the power that works in us,"

To top it up, Romans 8:11 says,

"But if the Spirit of Him who raised Jesus from the dead dwells in you, He who raised Christ from the dead will also give life to your mortal bodies through His Spirit who dwells in you."

No stronghold can stand against "the power that raised Jesus from the dead." DON'T DOUBT!! Rather DOUBT YOUR DOUBTS." Doctor Lester Sumrall would always conclude each broadcast with – "Feed your Faith and Starve your doubts to death!"

WE DO NOT OVERCOME THE STRONGHOLDS IN OUR OWN STRENGTH BUT THROUGH GOD'S ALMIGHTINESS

The stronghold is the devil's way of getting back at God and that coupled with God's love for the victim is why God is ready to help the victim to destroy every stronghold.

Our main text (2 Corinthians 10:4) says,

*"For the weapons of our warfare are not carnal but **mighty in God** for pulling down strongholds,"* (Emphasis mine)

This means we do not overcome the strongholds in our own strength but through God's almightiness. If we make a strong resolve to deal with those strongholds, and not doubt, God will come through and we will always emerge winners.

WE NEED, TRUE, GENUINE FORGIVENESS FROM THE HEART

CHAPTER 17

DESTROYING THE STRONGHOLD OF UNFORGIVENESS

Unforgiveness is a very stubborn stronghold. It can be so fortified that the victim can seize to see it as a stronghold. It becomes their lifestyle.

The stronghold says, "Why should I forgive them if they have not apologized to me?" Sometimes it says, "He must know that I am not okay after what he did to me." In other words the victim of the stronghold cannot forgive until the offender feels it. Even if the offender says sorry this victim has a way of "applying salt to the wound" for the offender to "REEEEEALY" feel that they offended them. It really has to soak in. I used to do this with my kids. When one of them messed up and I was mad at her she would try to talk to me and I would not answer or respond to her for her to "reeeealy" feel that she had messed up.

May I submit to you that when unforgiveness acts this way it becomes "A SUBTLE WAY OF REVENGE." The victim wants the offender to really feel the pain of remorse.

Sometimes people can be used by Satan in his endeavour to destroy us and unless we realise that its him and these people are just tools , unforgiveness can set in until it concretizes into a stronghold. If I use a book to strike you in the face you don't ask the book why it is striking you but you ask me. The book was just the tool I used. This understanding goes a long way in helping us forgive, especially in matters where forgiveness is so difficult.

Not all people who offend us are evil. Sometimes it's a one-off event. It's good to remember that in life we have also offended others. Appreciating this prevents a stronghold of unforgiveness from forming in our lives. Also, realizing that God has forgiven us from a seemingly unforgivable mess should be a great motivation for us to forgive. Jesus teaches it in Matthew 18:21-35. The Bible says,

"Then Peter came to Him and said, "Lord, how often shall my brother sin against me, and I forgive him? Up to seven times?" Jesus said to him, "I do not say to you, up to seven times, but up to seventy times seven. Therefore the kingdom of heaven is like a certain king who wanted to settle accounts with his servants. And when he had begun to settle accounts, one was brought to him who owed him ten thousand talents. But as he was not able to pay, his master commanded that he be sold, with his wife and children and all that he had, and that payment be made. The servant therefore fell down before him, saying, 'Master, have patience with me, and I will pay you all.' Then the master of that servant was moved with compassion, released him, and forgave him the debt. But that servant went out and found one of his fellow servants who owed him a hundred denarii; and he laid hands on him and took him by the throat, saying, 'Pay me what you owe!' So his fellow servant fell down at his feet and begged him, saying, 'Have patience with me, and I will pay you

all.' And he would not, but went and threw him into prison till he should pay the debt. So when his fellow servants saw what had been done, they were very grieved, and came and told their master all that had been done. Then his master, after he had called him, said to him, 'You wicked servant! I forgave you all that debt because you begged me. Should you not also have had compassion on your fellow servant, just as I had pity on you?' And his master was angry, and delivered him to the torturers until he should pay all that was due to him. "So My heavenly Father also will do to you if each of you, from his heart, does not forgive his brother his trespasses."

Forgiveness withheld for a long season become a stronghold. Another year a group of leaders, senior to me, teamed up and lied against me. It was painful. Did you know that, like we discussed earlier, a stronghold can be seen on a victim's face because it affects emotions. The people who were supposed to encourage me were destroying me. How could I accept their leadership? It was taking toll on me and was almost bordering on depression. Thank God for grace. As I was praying one day, the Holy Spirit gave me 2 Corinthians 4:7 which says,

"But we have this treasure in earthen vessels, that the excellence of the power may be of God and not of us."

The Holy Spirit explained to me that they had done this because they are earthen vessels but the leadership delegated to them is God's treasure. It was a powerful encounter. He reminded me that I was also an earthen vessel capable of earthen behaviour. It was then that it felt like a very dark cloud lifted up from me and I forgave all of them. By the way, none of

DO YOU KNOW THAT SOME CHRISTIANS ARE 'WALKING CEMETERIES?' THERE ARE OFFENDERS IN THEIR HEARTS WHO HAVE SINCE DIED BUT THEY HAVE NOT FORGIVEN THEM

them ever came to apologize to me even after it was exposed that they had lied against me. We don't forgive because someone has said they are sorry. We forgive because it's good for our spiritual and physical health.

Sometimes victims of abuse, especially sexual and physical abuse, find it tough to forgive and they end up having to deal with strongholds of unforgiveness and sometimes depression. It becomes complicated when they begin to ask questions like, "Why did God allow it?", "Why me, of all the people?" They end up having to forgive themselves (e.g. a rape victim may say, "maybe I was provocatively dressed or maybe I did not take necessary precautions or why did I agree to go with him".) They may also blame God (for supposedly allowing it) or the abuser. When the victim cannot feel justified or protected, they might even accuse God for allowing the incident to take place. It is a difficult struggle for the victim to place the blame on a moving target.

I have already prescribed part of the truth in that the abuse was used by the devil. It is important to know that evil occurs in this world because it is a "fallen world" with, "the ruler of this world/age" reigning in it. Satan is his name. 2 Corinthians 4:4 says,

"whose minds the god of this age has blinded, who do not believe, lest the light of the gospel of the glory of Christ, who is the image of God, should shine on them."

John 14:30 also says,

"I will no longer talk much with you, for the ruler of this world is coming, and he has nothing in Me."

God is not responsible. God is good. The devil is evil.

Luke 23:33-34 says,

"And when they had come to the place called Calvary, there they crucified Him, and the criminals, one on the right hand and the other on the left. 34 Then Jesus said, "Father, forgive them, for they do not know what they do.""

Jesus demonstrated true forgiveness. We also learn from Stephen. He says, in Acts 7:60, which says,

"Then he knelt down and cried out with a loud voice, "Lord, do not charge them with this sin." And when he had said this, he fell asleep."

We need, true, genuine forgiveness from the heart. The stronghold of unforgiveness must crumble down. Do you know that some Christians are 'walking cemeteries?' There are offenders in their hearts who have since died but they have not forgiven them. Unforgiveness, as a stronghold, is like a umbilical cord connecting the offender to the offended. Because of this connection the offender can remotely control the victim's life. How painful to know that some people's lives are being controlled from the graveyard where the unforgiven now lay. May God help us. Some Christians are carrying spooks inside them. This is because the people in their hearts, who died long ago, sometimes rise up in their minds and begin to offend the victim again and then he forgets it. The following day the person rises up again and the offense is replayed in the victim's mind

Did you know, you can wake up sad and moody just because you remembered the offense or the offender yet the offender may be thousands of miles away or even dead? Unforgiveness is a terrible root for many chronic diseases like cancer, hypertension, depression and many other psychotic diseases. After all, forgiveness helps me and not my offender. So why wait till they apologize or feel the remorse. They may never say, "I am sorry." They may never feel remorseful but we must forgive them for our sakes and the Lord's.

A CHILD WHO GROWS UP IN
AN ENVIRONMENT THAT IS
OPPRESSIVE OR INTIMIDATING
WILL DEVELOP INFERIORITY AND
LOW SELF-ESTEEM

CHAPTER 18

DESTROYING THE STRONGHOLD OF INFERIORITY COMPLEX AND LOW SELF-ESTEEM

A lot of the people God used greatly had to be delivered from this stronghold first. Sometimes God will speak through your inferiority complex and use you anyway. Moses was mightily used by God but he suffered from low self-esteem.

What did Moses say when God first told him about his assignment of delivering Israel from Egyptian slavery? Exodus 3:11 says,

"But Moses said to God, "who am I that I should go to Pharaoh, and that I should bring the children of Israel out of Egypt?""

In Jeremiah 1:5 – 6, Jeremiah had this to say:

"Then said I: "Ah, Lord God! Behold, I cannot speak, for I am a youth."

Despite God calling Gideon a mighty man of valour, listen to Gideon's response coming from a deep-seated stronghold of inferiority and low self-esteem. Judges 6:15 says,

"So he said to Him, 'O my Lord, how can I save Israel? Indeed my clan is the weakest in Manasseh, and I am the least in my father's house.'"

The list goes on and on. Jabez had to pray to be able to overcome inferiority. The stronghold of inferiority is a great limitation to what the victim can and must accomplish in life. It can hinder one's promotion. It can hamper one's business venture. Low self-esteem or inferiority can intimidate the victim from taking up opportunities that were meant to be their source of breakthrough into God's prosperity.

Listen to what Apostle Ezekiel Guti says in his book, Control your mind (back cover),

"Know that you are somebody. How can you enjoy in the Kingdom of God when you think there is someone more superior to you. The problem is in your mind. Don't live in fear but in knowledge. If you don't know how to rule your mind you are not going to be stable."

Usually the stronghold stems from a prolonged history of abuse, especially physical and verbal abuse. Poor handling of past failure is another root of inferiority. A child who grows up in an environment that is oppressive or intimidating will develop inferiority and low self-esteem. I know there are very loving step parents out there who raised up and nurtured children who were not biologically theirs but in my little counselling experience, the majority of cases involve children who grew up under abusive step parents. Sometimes it may not be a step parent but any guardian who takes up responsibility for the child. My wife testifies of how she stayed in a homestead where the children who belonged would have dinner with meat while she was given only vegetables, not because she was vegetarian. They would all be eating in the same room. Imagine the great damage it would do to a young kid. That is why at a later stage God had to deliver her from the stronghold of inferiority and low self-esteem.

Some feel inferior because of their race, educational level and even how they look. Coming from a different part of the world could make you feel inferior. But it is just geographical. Being black or white must not make you feel inferior. Even in the face of racism, brace up and tell yourself, "I am fearfully and wonderfully made." (Psalm 139:14)

Job says, in Job 13:2,

"What you know, I also know. I'm not inferior to you."

When God created man He created him in His own image. As men multiplied God just put them into differently-colored earthen houses called bodies. Some are white, some are black, some are brown but they were all made in the image of God. This is why I find racism insane. My father, Apostle Ezekiel Guti is well known worldwide for coining the statement, "People are people." You cannot control how people will speak to and treat you in a racist fashion but you can surely control how you respond to it and the level to which it affects you. Refuse to feel inferior.

Even if your background should make you feel inferior, you are not your background. You are who God says you are. Don't let your past define you. You are not inferior!

The other truth one needs in order to demolish this stronghold is to dig deep into its root. If it's abuse, forgive the abusers, and ask the Holy Spirit, through the Word, to heal your past emotional wounds. Negate every negative word that was

EVEN IF YOUR BACKGROUND SHOULD MAKE YOU FEEL INFERIOR, YOU ARE NOT YOUR BACKGROUND. YOU ARE WHO GOD SAYS YOU ARE. DON'T LET YOUR PAST DEFINE YOU. YOU ARE NOT INFERIOR!

said that brought inferiority by employing the truth of God's Word. Keep besieging that stronghold with Truth, keep firing a barrage of Truth until that stronghold of inferiority crumbles down.

You are not inferior. You have a Godly, high self-esteem in Jesus' name. You are not what they said or what they are saying. You are who God said and is still saying you are.

REJECTION

X

CHAPTER 19

DESTROYING THE STRONGHOLD OF REJECTION

Just like I explained in my other book, How to Understand and Receive Total deliverance, being rejected is not the problem. What leads to a spirit of rejection or its demonic house, the stronghold of rejection, is how you react to the experience of rejection. Rejection is painful because it attacks or impacts who we really are, our self -worth, our self-esteem, our person. It usually forms into a stronghold when the victim is subjected to rejection over a protracted period and has not been taught how to handle rejection and how to forgive the perpetrators of the rejection. This is especially true when someone or people who are meant to love, cherish and accept you become the perpetrators. Rejection from a stranger or just an acquaintance does not usually lead to a stronghold.

The unfortunate part is that, because of the very intense pain rejection causes, rejection may lead to various other types of strongholds as one tries to drown themself from that pain. The stronghold of rejection can give birth to different strongholds of addiction e.g. sexual addictions, as one seeks acceptance, pornography, shopping, depression, anxiety, anger etc. just to name a few. These can also give birth to different other strongholds. When strongholds multiply and the victim becomes helpless and frustrated, another very dangerous stronghold may be built - the suicidal stronghold.

The stronghold of rejection produces thoughts, feelings and actions that try to prevent further rejection. The victim exudes these feelings and subsequent actions without exerting any mental energy. It becomes normal and habitual. If left for a long time, most strongholds become habit and ultimately become character or behaviour. Let me give a few examples of the behavioural pattern of a person with a stronghold of rejection. The stronghold produces thoughts like,

"If only I can work my way to the top, at any cost, I will no longer be rejected. I will actually be the one who is well-positioned to reject others,"

"I have to lie or exaggerate my way out because if I am found guilty they will reject me again."

"I have to be in charge or in control of everyone and everything so that no one is able to reject me. When I am in a position of control it's me who has the ability to reject."

This leads to the "Jezebel" stronghold which houses the Jezebel spirit of control. The stronghold of rejection can also cause men- pleasing. The idea is you have to please everyone so that no one among them would reject you. The stronghold of rejection can also lead to a serious defensive mechanism just to prevent further rejection. The other tormenting thought from this stronghold of rejection pretty much treats everyone as a potential perpetrator of rejection. This affects relationships because you lose trust in anyone. This explains why victims of this stronghold specialize in rejecting others.

TELL YOUR MIND THAT THE LOVE OF GOD IN YOU CONSTRAINS YOU TO LOVE OTHERS. DECIDE TO LOVE OTHERS FIRST. MAKE UP YOUR MIND TO STARVE THAT STRONGHOLD BY STOPPING THE COMPENSATORY BEHAVIOR THAT IS COMING FROM THE STRONGHOLD OF REJECTION

It becomes even more disastrous if the spirit of rejection become housed in the stronghold of rejection. The spirit of rejection, camouflages the victim so that people don't see who they really are. They see someone fit to be rejected. This explains why victims of the stronghold of rejection become victims to victimization or false accusations. They are not able to receive love. The stronghold suggests that those who are giving them love have a hidden agenda. Their love is not real or genuine. The victims' ideas are always rejected but received when the same ideas come from other people. They develop a thorny character that drives people away. I call it the porcupine syndrome or the sandpaper syndrome. People end up with serious abrasions when they try to come close to people with a stronghold or spirit of rejection.

To pull the stronghold of rejection down, to demolish it, one must first go back to its roots, the initial experience of rejection, and receive healing from it. This healing is usually preceded by forgiving the perpetrators of the underlying rejection. This should be immediately done by besieging the mind with the Truth about God's love and acceptance of us. Psalm 27:10 says,

"When my father and my mother forsake me, then the Lord will take care of me."

Jeremiah 31:3 also says,

"The Lord has appeared of old to me, saying: 'Yes, I have loved you with an everlasting love; therefore with loving kindness I have drawn you.'"

Again the Bible says, in Ephesians 1:6,

"to the praise of the glory of His grace, by which He made us accepted in the Beloved."

Do away with the thought that everyone is a potential perpetrator of further rejection. Retrain the mind that you are lovable. The love of God in you makes you an object of love. Tell your mind that the love of God in you constrains you to love others. Decide to love others first. Make up your mind to starve that stronghold by stopping the compensatory behavior that is coming from the stronghold of rejection.

Because the stronghold of rejection, the stronghold of low self-esteem and the stronghold of inferiority are like triplets it becomes necessary to quickly fill one's mind with thoughts about who you are in Christ, what you are able to do in Christ and all Scriptures talking about God's love for you. You are not inferior. You are fearfully and wonderfully made. You can do all things through Christ who strengthens you. You are God's special "person." The Bible says, in 1 Peter 2:9,

"But you are a chosen generation, a royal priesthood, a holy nation, His own special people, that you may proclaim the praises of Him who called you out of darkness into His marvellous light;"

CHAPTER 20

DESTROYING THE STRONGHOLD OF GRIEF FROM LOSS

Loss of anything that is so dear can form a stronghold in one's mind but in this chapter I will begin with and put more emphasis on the loss of loved ones although I will touch a little bit on the other losses. In other words I will major on how to pull down the stronghold of grief from the bereaved. It is very common for a stronghold of grief to house a demon of grief if it is not quickly demolished.

Many years ago, in my culture, children were not allowed to attend funerals, let alone go to the cemetery. I now believe this was done to prevent the forming of this stronghold in their minds. This could be the reason why the Bible says, in 1 Thessalonians 4:13,

"But I do not want you to be ignorant, brethren, concerning those who have fallen asleep, lest you sorrow as others who have no hope."

The stronghold of grief forms when the victim loses a very close loved one to death and they cannot cope with the loss and fails to have the right help or counsel in time. This stronghold fills the victim with very tormenting anxiety of further loss. Every time the phone rings, the stronghold suggests that it is bad news about another loss. If the victim's spouse is delayed somewhere, the stronghold says they are dead. "Maybe it's an accident," the stronghold suggests. If one hears about an accident that has just happened, the stronghold suggests that one of the causalities is your loved one. Worse still, the stronghold makes you to lose the meaning of life and if uncurbed may lead to suicidal thoughts. Sometimes it may not result in suicidal thoughts but it can cause you to picture your own death and funeral. You lose sight of your future. You lose hope to live.

The stronghold fills your mind with what ifs' of loss. "What if so and so dies?", "What if my husband dies?", "What if my wife dies?", "What if my child dies?"

If this stronghold is not demolished in time it can ultimately lead to a stronghold more difficult to deal with - the stronghold of depression.

To pull down this stronghold one needs the proper Biblical concept of death. We should not try to understand and find answers for everything though. Deuteronomy 29:29 says,

"The secret things belong to the Lord our God, but those things which are revealed belong to us and to our children forever, that we may do all the words of this law."

There are some questions whose answers we will only get when we get to the other side of eternity. God allows some things, without causing them, for some reasons which are behind the scenes and which we may not know on this side of eternity.

A story is told of this group of Christians in the United States who prayed for a fellow ill Christian they loved dearly for nearly two years. That woman died anyway but they did not stop praying. This time they were asking God, "WHY?" After a long time of bombarding the throne of God with "WHY?" God felt pity for them and spoke, through one of them, something that was meant to be within His counsels, from his "behind the scenes". God said, "If this woman had lived two more years she was going to backslide."

Sometimes it is wise not to put a question mark where God has put a period (full stop). I believe one more example will drive the point home. It is said of William Branham that when he started to teach on the erroneous doctrine of the serpent seed and that he was the last messenger, the last prophet, God sent two men of God, at different times, to rebuke him, Oral Roberts and Kenneth Haggins. God said, "If you continue to teach this I am going to take your life to save your soul." He did not obey and in three months he was involved in a car crash and died. All the people at the funeral could have been crying, "Why God?" except the two men of God who had received their "behind the scenes" information from God.

Do you now see why we should not allow the stronghold of grief to set in and end up in depression by continuously asking God "Why?"

At this stage may I submit to you that God is not the causative effect in all of these deaths occurring in this world. We live in a fallen world in which Satan is the "god of this world." Some people need to forgive God before they can demolish the

IMAGINE HAVING LOST YOUR MIND AND YOU STILL HAVE FORTY MORE YEARS TO LIVE AFTER YOU LOSE YOUR DEAREST. DEAL WITH THE STRONGHOLD OF GRIEF. PULL IT DOWN!

stronghold of grief. Some people, when they mourn for the deceased, say, in the presence of some young people, "God has taken her! God has taken her!" To this young mind God becomes a cruel monster who took away their mother. A stronghold is built in their mind and they may never worship God in their life until they are taught and helped to demolish this stronghold.

It is also important for everyone to understand and accept that death has come into this world to stay. The Bible states, in Romans 5:12,

"Therefore, just as through one man sin entered the world, and death through sin, and thus death spread to all men, because all sinned-"

It is painful but true to say that all your loved ones and you too will one day pass on. This truth must be recorded in your "life and death" file. The important responsibility must be to work out one's life so that when that day comes one goes to be with the Lord. We all go the same way. Apostle E.H. Guti said, in 2010, when we were holding Jubilee celebrations for our church,

"Don't pray for me not to die but pray for me to accomplish all that God sent me to do. I am going to escort you in the next fifty years and I will disappear along the way." It is a declaration from someone who has no fear of death. It is typical of great men and women of God. Paul says, in Acts 21:13,

"Then Paul answered, "What do you mean by weeping and breaking my heart? I am ready not only to be bound, but also to die at Jerusalem for the name of the Lord Jesus."

Peter also said, in 2 Peter 1:14,

"knowing that shortly I must put off my tent, just as our Lord Jesus Christ showed me."

Paul again says, in Philippians 1:21 – 24,

"For to me, to live is Christ, and to die is gain. But if I leave on in the flesh, this will mean fruit from my labour; yet what I shall choose I cannot tell. For I am hard-pressed between the two, having a desire to depart and be with Christ, which is far better. Nevertheless to remain in the flesh is more needful for you."

To pull down the stronghold of grief, choose scriptures of hope and besiege your mind with those Scriptures. Psalm 118:17 says,

"I shall not die, but live and declare the works of the Lord."

When you lose a loved one it is not a suggestion that you are going to die tomorrow. Allow the Holy Spirit to heal you from the loss and to strengthen you to trudge on into the future. Whoever they were in your life, God still has a way of having you fulfil your destiny now that they are gone. When a "Moses" dream dies God always has a "Joshua" dream for you. There is a hope in God for you. There is life after loss and you still need your mind for living. Don't give it up to grief. Imagine having lost your mind and you still have forty more years to live after you lose your dearest. Deal with the stronghold of grief. Pull it down!

Do you know of people who still weep and grieve over the death of a loved one on the 30th anniversary of their death. They weep and grieve every day a special date they lived with the deceased comes around: their wedding day, their birthday, all special events they experienced together with the deceased. This can continue for many years! Pull down that stronghold.

Those who lose their spouses and give in to the stronghold of grief will forever suffer from its torment even if they remarry. It will cause them to compare the new spouse with their late spouse, thirty or more years down the line. May God help us.

Sometimes telling the mind over and over again that if I love the Lord I will meet my loved one again can bring healing and help pull down the stronghold of grief. Keep pumping the Truth of God's Word into your mind. Tell your mind of how people you know have also lost their loved ones but God has strengthened them and they are moving on, fulfilling their destinies. Allow yourself, give yourself up to the healing virtue of the Holy Spirit. It is important to recognize the existence of the stronghold of grief in your life and have mature people speak into you. It also helps to have people interceding for you. This is because for some, when they are under the spirit of grief, it becomes difficult to pray or read and understand the Word of God. Actually the stronghold begins to bring in thoughts that say, "Do you think God really exists? Why would he allow such a thing to happen?"

I tried share about Christ to this man. He blatantly said to me, "There is no one up there!" meaning to say there is no God up there. After a deep conversation with him I learnt he had lost his only son and only child two years before in a car crash. This is what a stronghold of grief can do. Have you watched that movie, "God is not dead." The professor was suffering under the stronghold of grief. As a man who had lived as a Christian, he really, deep down in his heart, knew that God was real but he tried to drown himself from the pain of the loss of his mother by being a proponent of the notion that God does not exist, He is dead. Many atheists of our day fell into this trap and if many of them can be helped to pull down the stronghold of grief, they may end up born again. Deuteronomy 34:8 says,

"And the children of Israel wept for Moses in the plains of Moab thirty days. So the days of weeping and mourning for Moses ended."

Tell your mind I will mourn but it must end. The stronghold of grief will paralyze you in your pursuit to fulfill your purpose. Sometimes it condemns you as if you are responsible for the death. It says,

"Maybe if I had taken her to this hospital,"

"It was me who asked him to go buy groceries and the crash occurred,"

"Had I not left my child alone,"

"I should have counselled her enough before the suicide."

The stronghold keeps pumping these thoughts into your conscious mind and it is so tormenting. Tell your mind, this day comes to all and no one can pass their day. One year, when my brother-in-law was ill with the illness that took him to be with the Lord, my spiritual father, Archbishop Ezekiel Guti, strengthened my wife and I with these deep words, "Sickness is not death but death is all about time."

The same thing is true with that car crash. It was about time which was up, it was not the crash. This is why some escape crashes and people look at the car and conclude that no one survived. Some people spend months in the CCU or ICU and one day you meet them jogging while at the same time someone may complain about a headache for an hour and they die. It is time. You are not the cause. Tell your mind over and over again that it is about time. It is not really those people. It is time. If you don't tell your mind this truth you will end up blaming people for the loss and blaming yourself for the loss. They could have been used as channels but remember it is time that kills!! Not only time but the devil "comes to steal, to kill and to destroy..." (John 10:10)

THE MIND IS LIKE A MOTOR (CAR ENGINE)..
IF IT IS RUN WITH NO OIL IT WILL KNOCK
OFF.. IT JUST CEASES.. IT JUST SHUTS
DOWN. IT , OF COURSE, GIVES WARNING
SIGNS BUT IF THESE WARNING SIGNS
ARE IGNORED IT JUST SHUTS OFF.. THIS IS
WHAT THE MIND DOES WITH DEPRESSION.

CHAPTER 21

DESTROYING THE STRONGHOLD OF DEPRESSION AND ANXIETY

Depression is a very complex condition to deal with. To begin with, some of the causes of this mental health issue are beyond the victim's control. They could be biological causes, generic causes and sometimes from medication. It is a well proven medical fact that the medication for acne can cause depression. Have you ever heard of post-natal depression? It is beyond the victim's control. All these are not caused by anything the victim does. Some hormonal imbalances can cause depression, for example excessive release of cortisol can lead to depression.

In this discussion I will lean more on the causes that stem from what the victim does, doesn't do or goes through.

Depression comes when a victim is incessantly asking questions of life but have no answers. It comes when a victim is trying to change situations they cannot change. Failure to deal with shame and when people reject you for what you did can be a great cause of depression. It's compounded when people judge and condemn you for that thing. This is why people who fail and are condemned end up suicidal. Sometimes bad news from doctors can cause depression and anxiety. People who are diagnosed with terminal diseases can end up depressed. It's powerful to know that God always has the final answer and not the doctor. This is why, today, we have people who were given six months to live but have been alive for more than twenty years now and are as strong as horses. We prayed with a woman who was given a few days to live but it's now five years and she is alive and strong. A stronghold of that kind can kill you before you die – in your mind.

It can also be a result of doing something for a long time but yielding no results. In this case depression is birthed from untreated burnout that goes on for a protracted length of time.

When the mind is overwhelmed it can shut down and that is the extreme end of depression. The mind is like a motor (car engine). If it is run with no oil it will knock off. It just ceases. It just shuts down. It, of course, gives warning signs but if these warning signs are ignored it just shuts off. This is what the mind does with depression.

Remember, in the chapter we dealt with strongholds that come from loss, I indicated that undealt-with grief will ultimately mature into depression. Some people who lose jobs, houses, marriages, relationships, money, loved ones etc. may recede into depression as long as they don't receive quick and effective counsel. Also, victims of abuse can end up depressed if they don't get quick help. Failure to handle failure is another cause of the stronghold of depression. Worry and anxiety experienced over a long time is another ardent cause of depression. The feeling of guilt is yet another cause. Fighting to be in control of something that is now out of control may

THE HOLY SPIRIT SPECIALIZES IN INNER HEALING. HE IS EXPERT IN HEALING PAST WOUNDS AND IN HELPING US UNDERSTAND WHAT WE CANNOT NATURALLY UNDERSTAND. WHEN A VICTIM OF DEPRESSION JUST OPENS UP TO THE HOLY SPIRIT, IN PRAYER, HE WILL BRING THE HEALING

land one in the pit of depression. We should not try to control things which God only can control.

There are several indicators that there is a stronghold of depression or anxiety that must be demolished from a victim's life or mind. Here are some of them:

- ☑ A desire to be left alone, craving isolation. A victim of depression or anxiety can shut himself up in a house for a long time. Sometimes they can shut themselves in without bathing, cleaning up, eating and sometimes over eating.
- ☑ Signs of memory failure, usually short term memory and sometimes frequent episodes of blankness of mind.
- ☑ Sleep disorder - Either lack of sleep or continuous sleep.
- ☑ Fatigue – victims can experience tiredness that cannot be explained.
- ☑ Loss of interest in things they used to have pleasure in.
- ☑ Loss of creativity and innovativeness.
- ☑ Suicidal thoughts – if this is not dealt with on time victims of depression may actually end up taking the lives.
- ☑ Mood swings – depression can result in a bipolar behaviour.
- ☑ Increased irritability
- ☑ Self-harming.
- ☑ Emotional imbalance etc.

In order to demolish the stronghold of depression it is requisite that one digs deep to the initial cause or event the reaction to which deteriorated into depression. Unless that root is addressed first, it could be very difficult to demolish the stronghold.

It's amazing that healing can sometimes begin when the victim simply writes down their real testimony. Not the doctored, sensored testimonies we give in church. E.g. I was raped, molested, rejected, abused etc. This helps because this breaks the barrier of denial that hinders one's healing. Never camouflage pain. Pour it out. When you have gone through something you never shared with anyone sometimes you can't think straight. Even Jesus had to pour out His pain when He was in the garden of Gethsemane. Matthew 26:36-39 says,

"Then Jesus came with them to a place called Gethsemane, and said to the disciples, "Sit here while I go and pray over there." And He took with Him Peter and the two sons of Zebedee, and He began to be sorrowful and deeply distressed. Then He said to them, "My soul is exceedingly sorrowful, even to death. Stay here and watch with Me." He went a little farther and fell on His face, and prayed, saying, "O My Father, if it is possible, let this cup pass from Me; nevertheless, not as I will, but as You will."

Sometimes it takes forgiveness as we address the past, especially if the cause was something that was done against us. The Holy Spirit specializes in inner healing. He is expert in healing past wounds and in helping us understand what we cannot naturally understand. When a victim of depression just opens up to the Holy Spirit, in prayer, He will bring the healing. I know, in such moments, prayer may be difficult. Just give your heart to Him in faith. He will minister to you. Open up to new truth in the area that may have caused the depression.

CONSTANT EXPOSURE TO PORNOGRAPHIC MATERIAL CAN RESULT IN A STRONGHOLD OF LUST.. WE MUST ALWAYS GUARD OUR MINDS..

CHAPTER 22

DESTROYING SEXUAL STRONGHOLDS

1 Thessalonians 4:3-5 says,
"For this is the will of God, your sanctification: that you should abstain from sexual immorality; 4 that each of you should know how to possess his own vessel in sanctification and honor, 5 not in passion of lust, like the Gentiles who do not know God;"

In this chapter I have bundled all strongholds that are related to the sexual sins or tendencies.

Stronghold of Lust

We really understand that lust can be a giant in one's flesh. It can be part of one's sinful nature or the works of the flesh or the deeds of the body. Paul admonishes us to "work out our salvation." (Philippians 2:12) Lust can also be iniquity. Iniquity is sin but usually generational sin that follows the bloodline. That can be dealt with by breaking generational curses, as we discussed in Spiritual Warfare 1.

In this chapter, however, we are dealing with lust as a stronghold. Usually it can be recognised by wayward sexual thoughts emanating from the stronghold. One can look at anything and always see it from a sexual perspective; a car, a tree, a dog, a woman, a man, a cow etc. I mean anything. That's how bad a stronghold of lust can be. Nothing goes by the victim without the mind relating it to sex. Have you ever wondered why in our day even a car can be called "sexy." That word is being wrongly used and is being overused.

Sexual wayward thoughts can be very tormenting and frustrating especially when the victim is unaware of the operation of strongholds. One can end up beating up themselves for thinking those thoughts and usually uncontrollably. The victim's mind can undress and sleep with anyone of the opposite sex who comes before them. Worse still, this can happen in church while someone of the opposite sex (or same sex for some fighting feelings from the alternative lifestyle) is doing something in the house of the Lord.

This stronghold sets in sometimes when someone had a bad sexual experience, especially in early childhood. Maybe one was exposed to pornography at a tender age. Sexual molestation can also open that door. Constant exposure to pornographic material can result in a stronghold of lust. We must always guard our minds. In today's world, they are subtly introducing the unsuspecting people to soft porn. It comes in commercials or advertisements. Even a car is now described as sexy. The word sexy is now being used to describe, pretty much, anything. A scantily dressed woman has become a norm on many commercials in our day. For a music show to be well attended and for the music to sell, it seems like the musician has to be scantily or provocatively dressed and they have to dance suggestively, provocatively and promiscuously for the show to be "successful and enjoyable." Such is the world in which we are supposed to live and exhibit "the mind of Christ." (1 Corinthians 2:16)

We meet scantily dressed women in the streets, at school, at the mall, at the hospital, on the bus, on the plane, on the train, at work, and surprisingly at church. Mini-skirts or mini-dresses are the norm, in real life or on television. Revealing tops (with breasts showing – they call it cleavage) are the order of the day. It's no longer about porn sites or "adult" shows and clubs only. They can bring it right into your house and even on kids' channels. The only way to escape is to deal with one's mind. Apostle Guti always speaks about being saved or being born again in your mind. As long as you are in this world you cannot run away. Tell and retrain your mind that only your wife or husband should appeal to you sexually. Tell it over and over again. As it becomes habit, your body will follow your mind and before you know it those pictures and those women or men become disgusting to look at because where your mind goes your life goes.

If your mind insists on desiring to see those explicit pictures and you are married, I have a good, effective and useful piece of advice for you. Get into your bedroom and ask your wife or husband to undress. If you were keen to look lustfully at women's legs, guess what? Your wife has legs too. If you are single tell your mind, "NOT NOW!!" It's all in the mind. My mentor, Dr. E.H. Guti, teaches us to consider the older women as our mothers, women of our age as our sisters and the younger girls as our daughters. For woman we need to treat older men

YOU NEED TO TELL YOUR MIND THAT "WE OBEY THE WORD OF GOD." EXPLAIN TO YOUR MIND THAT JESUS SAID LUST IS ADULTERY, SO WE WILL NOT LOOK AT A WOMEN OR MAN LUSTFULLY

as our fathers, men of same age as brothers and younger men as sons. If we can retrain our minds this way we can overcome the stronghold of lust.

We spoke about mustering or being in charge of internal dialogue that takes place as thoughts leave the subconscious mind into your conscious mind. Learn to confront the lustful thoughts. Ask them questions like, "Why should we waste time and energy looking at women we will not sleep with. After all we cannot sleep with all the women in the world." Women should address their thoughts the same way when lustful thoughts are demanding attention. Job says, in Job 31:1,

"I have made a covenant with my eyes; why then should I look upon a young woman?"

If you are a woman just replace young woman by "young man" and the Scripture remains the same.

You need to tell your mind that "we obey the Word of God." Explain to your mind that Jesus said lust is adultery, so we will not look at a women or man lustfully. Also tell your mind that your wife, if you are married, or your future wife, if unmarried, has the same things that your mind wants you to look at on other women. If the stronghold wants you to look at other women's breasts, tell your mind, "Those breasts belong to her, her child or her husband." If you are a young, unmarried man tell your mind, "I will look at my wife when I get married, it's too early to look at other women." Young, unmarried women should say the same to their minds about looking lustfully at men.

Learn to speak back to those lustful thoughts and sooner or later your mind is retrained and you'll have pulled down the stronghold of lust.

The Stronghold of Pornography

If a child is exposed to or lives in an environment where pornography is watched they can grow up bound by this addiction. Some are lured into it by friends and for some they stumble into it on the internet. For those who already have a demon of lust, the demon drives them into it. If someone struggling with lust already stumbles onto some naked pictures they may be tempted to look for more and for deeper. These days, seductive pictures or videos are scattered all over common internet pages like Yahoo or Google homepages. They are just lightly suggestive but they will have links to the real thing. The same pictures are thrown all over on the social media. The dangerous sites will just be a single click away. You need grace between your computer mouse and your finger to escape.

The world has become a sexual predator. But if the mind has been retrained, this poses no threat. We helped one girl who was so bound by this stronghold that she would wake up every 2 O'clock in the morning to watch pornography. It is so addictive and irresistible and the devil harnesses it easily to build other tenacious strongholds like masturbation, adultery or fornication.

The porn industry is a multi-billion industry. What people see there is not a real sexual experience. All is played out to make money and the devil promotes it to have more people in bondage. The lie of the devil is that, you can use it to spice up your marriage, BUT the truth is that it doesn't work. It's all fake. It's meant to raise money using innocent victims. Tell your mind it's not real. Tell your mind it's evil and it doesn't please God. Tell your mind it has been medically proven that dwelling on pornography dulls the victim's mind. No one indulges in it and remains with a sharp mind. You occasionally experience a blank mind. As you keep retraining your mind it begins to abhor the practice too. Substitute thoughts that pull you there by other Godly thoughts. Keep your mind busy with the right thoughts. The moment you begin to think pornography engage your mind with something profitable and Godly. Just get yourself busy. You can read the Bible, pray or listen to good music. Sooner or later your mind is retrained and pornography becomes history.

But there is some work to do. It is not as easy as eating. Read the chapter on how to overcome addictions. God gives "greater grace" for you to overcome the addictive stronghold of pornography. Usually if this stronghold is not dealt with, it will lead to another stronghold of masturbation.

Stronghold of Musturbation

After one has spent some time watching pornography, sexual tension results and in the absence of someone to have sex with, one would resort to masturbation. This is really addictive and can easily develop into a stronghold if not quickly overcome. The lie on which the stronghold is built is that it is not sinful because I am not committing adultery with no one. Those who practice it or have once indulged in it say that one has to engage in a lot of sexual fantasies or imaginations for it to work. You have to imagine having sex with some real person or meditate on some pornographic stuff one would have watched. Already this means you cannot separate musturbation and lust. Jesus equates lust to adultery and fornication.

Stronghold of Hormosexuality

Homosexuality is the sexual sin of men having a sexual relationship with another man or a woman with another woman. Some of the lies that are used to build the stronghold are:

i. I was born with this sexual inclination. It is my nature. I am a woman in a man's body or I am a man in a woman's body.

ii. It is a weakness just like adultery or fornication.

iii. No one can go to hell for being homosexual.

iv. I can also minister to God being homosexual. This explains why we are now having gay and lesbian pastors, especially in the United States.

God never created anyone with homosexual feelings. His anger against the inhabitants of Sodom and Gomorrah is a clear indication that it was never God's intention from the beginning. (Genesis 18 and 19) The same lifestyle is vehemently castigated in Romans 1:24-28. The Bible says,

DO YOU THINK GOD COULD HAVE DESTROYED SODOM AND GOMORRAH FOR THIS SIN? UP TO NOW THE SIN OF HOMOSEXUALITY IS ALSO CALLED SODOMY. IN ROMANS ONE, THE BIBLE SAYS "GOD GAVE THEM OVER TO A DEPRAVED MIND." THE NEW KING VERSION CALLS IT A DEBASED MIND

"Therefore God also gave them up to uncleanness, in the lusts of their hearts, to dishonor their bodies among themselves, who exchanged the truth of God for the lie, and worshiped and served the creature rather than the Creator, who is blessed forever. Amen. For this reason God gave them up to vile passions. For even their women exchanged the natural use for what is against nature. Likewise also the men, leaving the natural use of the woman, burned in their lust for one another, men with men committing what is shameful, and receiving in themselves the penalty of their error which was due. And even as they did not like to retain God in their knowledge, God gave them over to a debased mind, to do those things which are not fitting;"

Verse 28 suggests that the one who practices homosexuality has a **debased mind** and also equates it to **"doing those things which are not fitting."**

This stronghold is so binding and sometimes covenantal which makes it so difficult to demolish. The first huddle is to convince the victim that it is an abomination, because those involved don't see it that way. Actually, they think that those who condemn them are wrong and are acting out of hate.

Several cases of lesbianism I have met were of girls who never experienced a mother's love. Now this other woman comes into this girl's life and woes her into the sinful relationship and offers her the kind of love she missed. This result is a perverted mother-daughter relationship. As you know, a mother – daughter relationship is always meant to be strong. This explains why the resultant lesbian relationship is so strong and hard to break. This is a great warning to abusive mothers or mothers with no time to love their daughters. It's actually selling them over to this alternative lifestyle. It's also an eye-opener to counsellors who intend to help those girls. You have to show her motherly love that surpasses what she is experiencing in that lesbian relationship. I want to believe the same phenomena may happen to a boy who grows lacking or deprived of fatherly love. They will "find it" in that gay relationship.

I am still trying to come to terms with the possibility of someone being born with gay inclinations because the parents kept saying he was a girl while he was still a pregnancy or vice versa. It happens with parents who wait to know the gender of the child in the labour room while meanwhile they assume the child is of the gender they have been desiring. Sometimes it's assumed to be an act of faith. I think is safer to know the gender before time. I am just provoking your mind. I am not emphatically saying this is what happens. I am just thinking aloud. There are studies going on, on child development, that suggest that during the later stages of the foetus's development the foetus can hear and be affected by what is happening or being said externally. They call it phoneme contraction. Just food for thought.

To demolish this stronghold, it is important to refer the victim to Genesis 18 and 19 and Romans 1. If people were born with the homosexual nature or inclination, do you think God could have destroyed Sodom and Gomorrah for this sin? Up to now the sin of homosexuality is also called sodomy. In Romans

THE FIRST STEP IN OVERCOMING SEXUAL STRONGHOLDS AS A BELIEVER IN JESUS CHRIST IS TO RECOGNIZE WHO YOU ARE. YOU ARE A SAINT — WASHED, SANCTIFIED, AND JUSTIFIED

one, the Bible says "God gave them over to a **depraved** mind." The New King version calls it a **debased** mind.

In Romans 1:26-27, the Message Bible says,

"Worse followed. Refusing to know God, they soon didn't know how to be human either—women didn't know how to be women, men didn't know how to be men. Sexually confused, they abused and defiled one another, women with women, men with men—all lust, no love. And then they paid for it, oh, how they paid for it—emptied of God and love, godless and loveless wretches."

Keep repeating the Truth from Genesis and Romans 1 until the mind of the victim registers that it is a sin and an abomination before the Lord. Then apply the tips on dealing with addictive strongholds in Chapter 23. Once the mind has shifted it is very expedient to cut all relationships that involves meeting with other homosexual people. It means stopping going to their clubs. It means breaking away from all "love affairs" from that alternative lifestyle.

The anointing of God can demolish this kind of stronghold as long as there has been a mental shift and a desire to break away.

1Thessalonians 4:3-5 says,

"For this is the will of God, your sanctification: that you should abstain from sexual immorality; that each of you should know how to possess his own vessel in sanctification and honor, not in passion of lust, like the Gentiles who do not know God;"

1Corinthians 6:9-11 also says,

"Do you not know that the unrighteous will not inherit the kingdom of God? Do not be deceived. Neither fornicators, nor idolaters, nor adulterers, nor homosexuals, nor sodomites, nor thieves, nor covetous, nor drunkards, nor revilers, nor extortioners will inherit the kingdom of God. 11 And such were some of you. But you were washed, but you were sanctified, but you were justified in the name of the Lord Jesus and by the Spirit of our God."

Tony Evans says (Victory in Spiritual Warfare – page 203),

"The first step in overcoming sexual strongholds as a believer in Jesus Christ is to recognize who you are. You are a saint – washed, sanctified, and justified. You have a new identity now. When you keep that truth at the forefront of your mind, eventually the craving for whatever behaviour you were doing will begin to have less and less control over you because it does not line up with who you are. You will be functioning first and foremost out of your identity in Christ."

1 Corinthians 6:12-13 gives us our perspective. It says,

"All things are lawful for me, but all things are not helpful. All things are lawful for me, but I will not be brought under the power of any. Foods for the stomach and the stomach for foods, but God will destroy both it and them. Now the body is not for sexual immorality but for the Lord, and the Lord for the body."

When we view our bodies through God's perspective – that He made them for Him and that He is also there for us – then whatever we will do sexually needs to reflect His will and design. We are not our own.

How you view yourself pulls down the strongholds more than turning off the TV or internet or keeping yourself away from any tempting situation, person or location.

Also remember, if God has enough power to raise Jesus Christ from the dead, friend, He has enough power to give you the strength to resist and flee from sexual temptation. The solution is found by turning to him, replacing your own thoughts about who you are with His thoughts, and trusting Him to deliver you. When you operate under the truth of being "one spirit with him", the craving within you for an illegitimate expression of your sexuality will diminish and you will find strength to redirect your passions and desires towards the manifestation of a pure pleasure and satisfaction.

CHAPTER 23

DESTROYING ADDICTIVE STRONGHOLDS

There is a very wide range of such strongholds and these include chemical addictions, sexual addictions, food addictions, social media addictions, and shopping addictions, just to mention a few.

The main building block for all of these strongholds is the lie that one can fix an underlying problem using all the temporal fixes mentioned above. The other lie the devil uses is that one cannot live without those addictions. One will do it continually until it becomes a stronghold. One stronghold will lead into another until there are more to deal with. Doing all those ugly, quick fix and temporal activities can be likened to a young man who got rejected by a girlfriend just before their wedding day and had a terrible heartbreak. As a solution the young man bandaged his chest, exactly where the heart is.

When circumstances or the people around us bring us pain and anguish, causing us to feel beaten down, burdened, lonely or stressed, we reach for a quick fix to provide relief to a long term problem – alcohol, cigarette, pill or any other chemical infused into our body. This does not provide the strength or victory we seek.

This leads to a chemical stronghold – a dependency on chemicals to address, escape or cope with, or find relief from the struggles and stresses of life. Someone may say, "I just need a drink to unwind," or "I just need a smoke to reduce the stress."

It is absurd to begin to take drugs as a way of dealing with a stressful or depressing situation. Some will use food, sex, smoking, or shopping to drown themselves from pain.

To demolish such strongholds the first step would be to look back to the root. What was it that caused one to seek rescue from drugs or alcohol. For example, what type of pain was he or she trying to sedate themself from? James 4:7 says,

"Therefore submit to God. Resist the devil and he will flee from you."

There are two sides to submission; surrender and commitment. First you have to surrender. You have to acknowledge you can't deal with the addiction. You have tried and failed. Now you are surrendering to God to help you overcome it. The next step is now committing to overcome the addiction through the ability God only can give. Once God is in the picture, no addiction can stand against or resist God. Isaiah 43:13 says,

"Indeed before the day was, I am He; and there is no one who can deliver out of My hand; I work, and who will reverse it?"

Another version says,? ".. I work and who can hinder me"

Romans 8:11 says,

"But if the Spirit of Him who raised Jesus from the dead dwells in you, He who raised Christ from the dead will also give life to your mortal bodies through His Spirit who dwells in you."

No addiction can withstand the power that raised Jesus from the dead. James 4:6 also says,

"But He gives more grace. Therefore He says: 'God resists the proud, but gives grace to the humble.'"

I like the version that says, "**...greater grace**" God gives greater grace!! No matter how strong that addiction is, God gives greater grace. He gives greater grace! It doesn't matter what your mess is in life, how bad you were raised or what abuse you went through. I am not saying it didn't affect you or it wasn't serious. All I am saying is God gives greater grace. There is more grace, greater grace than your mess. Maybe you are saying, "I was abused." There is greater grace. Someone maybe saying, "I have been addicted for years." He gives greater grace!

To break the addictive stronghold, repeatedly tell your mind that God can make you live without drugs, alcohol, smoking etc. This helps to destroy the lie that you can't survive without getting high. Once the mind changes, the systems in your body will follow. Also, like we said in Chapter 10, stop feeding the stronghold. Starve it. As long as you begin the battle in the mind, you can stop getting drugs. Go where they are not available. Do away with drinking friends. Break away from wrong sexual relationships. Stop all activities that the addictive stronghold used to cause you to do. You can do it. God has "**greater grace**" available to you. Romans 5:20 says,

"Moreover the law entered that the offense might abound. But where sin abounded, grace abounded **much more**,"

There is grace that abounds much more than the stronghold. God gives grace that abounds much more.

THE ACTION OF TAKING DRUGS IS NOT THE PROBLEM. THE ACTION IS SIMPLY A MANIFESTATION OF THE PROBLEM. THE PROBLEM IS IN THE MIND. AND WHEN WE ALLOW GOD'S THOUGHTS – HIS SPIRIT – TO BE THE DOMINATING FORCE IN OUR LIVES, HE CHANGES EVERYTHING

When somebody is fighting to overcome chemical addiction do not call them a drug addict. Once they are born again, they are blood-bought children of the living God, and they have already been given victory over drugs. Tony Evans, in his book, Victory in Spiritual Warfare (page 189), says,

"The action of taking drugs is not the problem. The action is simply a manifestation of the problem. The problem is in the mind. And when we allow God's thoughts – His Spirit – to be the dominating force in our lives, He changes everything."

When you feel trapped in an addiction or by a habit, it's easy to forget that God has put a life line in each of our lives. He is just waiting for us to pick up the phone and give Him a call – PRAYER !!

The victim needs the Truth of the Word of God. 1 Corinthians 7:23 says,

"You were bought at a price; do not become slaves of men."

The Bible also says, in Romans 8:1-2,

"There is therefore now no condemnation to those who are in Christ Jesus, who do not walk according to the flesh, but according to the Spirit. For the law of the Spirit of life in Christ Jesus has made me free from the law of sin and death."

Again Romans 12:1-2 says,

"I beseech you therefore, brethren, by the mercies of God, that you present your bodies a living sacrifice, holy, acceptable to God, which is your reasonable service. And do not be conformed to this world, but be transformed by the renewing of your mind, that you may prove what is that good and acceptable and perfect will of God."

MARRIAGE IS A POWERFUL UNION AND IT MUST BE CONSIDERED THUS OR ELSE DIVORCEES WILL ALWAYS LIVE TO REGRET

CHAPTER 24

DESTROYING MARITAL STRONGHOLDS

Divorces frequently occur as a result of a stronghold in the way marriage is viewed e.g. if one has a wrong purpose or reason for marriage. When a man grows up without a mother and he gets married and expects his wife to fill the mother's role he missed growing up, the purpose of that marriage is very wrong. He can end up placing unachievable expectations on his wife. In the same vein, a woman who grew up without a father may also expect her husband to fill her father's role. She will end up frustrated as her husband fails to fill her father's shoes. To break that stronghold, we need to align our thoughts in keeping with God's viewpoint of a biblical, covenantal marriage.

Like we said, the marriage that was modeled before you, that was taught to you or that you experienced, maybe in a first marriage, can be a stronghold in your mind and you would expect your marriage to look like the one in your mind. This explains why people who grew up in the environment of an abusive marriage can end up in an abusive marriage or do the opposite extreme of spoiling their spouses. If curse words were the norm in the modeled marriage, curse words will be the norm in their marriage. A mother who disrespects her husband can sow seeds in a daughter that will cause her to also disrespect her husband. The same thing can affect a son and he will end up doing what he saw his father or guardian do.

This stronghold can affect every other aspect of marriage including how monetary issues are handled in the home. Communication, how in-laws are handled, sexual matters, etc. can all be affected by strongholds in either husband or wife.

A person in a second marriage can have a stronghold that can adversely affect the current marriage. There is a danger of interpreting everything one's spouse does or says based on what was happening in the first marriage or prior marriages. Sometimes it will lead to one having super expectations imposed on their spouse based on comparison with prior marriage(s).

Sometimes such strongholds can cause a girl to never want to get married. The lies will be, "All men are like what I have experienced. So why should I be married?" Divorce can cause one to say, "I will never open my heart like that again." This can cause problems if they remarry. To demolish such strongholds a couple must seek the truth of what a true, Scriptural, Christian and covenantal marriage should be like and incessantly feed that into their minds. Some strongholds will cause the victims to view the marriage covenant so casually and they will end up divorcing without giving thought to the dire consequences of divorce on their spouses, children, families, people around them and on themselves as individuals.

Marriage is a powerful union and it must be considered thus or else divorcees will always live to regret. One needs to realign his or her thoughts in keeping with God's viewpoint of a covenantal marriage. We discussed about Soul Ties in Spiritual Warfare 2. These have to be dealt with and destroyed because they are typical strongholds.

On another note, Apostle Ezekiel Guti once taught about the dangers of another form of marital strongholds; an overwhelming desire to get married. This has made victims to always think about marriage and developing sexual thoughts that have led a lot to begin to have "spiritual husbands." There is nothing wrong in desiring to be married but when the thought of it becomes possessive and overarching, then it becomes a stronghold.

"WE NEED MONEY HERE, NOT IN HEAVEN. THERE ARE STREETS OF GOLD IN HEAVEN. WE NEED TO DEAL WITH THE POVERTY MENTALITY."

CHAPTER 25

DESTROYING THE STRONGHOLD OF POVERTY

This is one of the most difficult strongholds to demolish. Sometimes it is related to a generational curse of poverty. The lie that builds it would be like, "Moreover no one else in my family or clan became rich. This is who we are." The other lie comes from misunderstanding and misquoting 1Timothy 6:10. The Bible does not say "money is the root of all evil." Rather it says,

"For the love of money is a root of all kinds of evil, for which some have strayed from the faith in their greediness, and pierced themselves through with many sorrows."

It says **the love of money** is the root of all evil. It does not say money is the root of all evil.

I grew up in Africa, in Zimbabwe, which was then Rhodesia. The Missionaries who brought the Bible to us, during the colonial era, told us that there was no problem in being poor because we were going to be rich in heaven. The gist of the teaching was that poverty would make one more godly. A lot of Christians misunderstand Matthew 19:24. The Bible says,

"And again I say to you, it is easier for a camel to go through the eye of a needle than for a rich man to enter the kingdom of God."

It is said that a gate exists in Israel which is actually called "the eye of a needle." This scripture refers to rich people who get rich using their own evil means. It does not refer to the people whom God makes rich. Abraham was rich but it was God who made him rich and as we speak he is enjoying in the Kingdom of Heaven. Isaac, Jacob, David and many other men of God in the Bible were extremely rich and they are in heaven right now as we speak. If all rich people don't go to heaven then why are these patriarchs there? The Book says, in Psalms 35:27,

"Let them shout for joy and be glad, who favour my righteous cause; and let them say continually, 'Let the Lord be magnified, who has pleasure in the prosperity of His servant.'"

God has pleasure in our prosperity. The Amplified Bible says,

"..., who delights and takes pleasure in the prosperity of His servant."

Remember, it is God who gives us the power to obtain wealth. Deuteronomy 8:18 says,

"And you shall remember the Lord your God, for it is He who gives you power to get wealth, that He may establish His covenant which He swore to your fathers, as it is this day."

All these scriptures do not suggest that God does not want us to be rich. A wrong mind-frame or concept about money or those who have money can build a stronghold of poverty in the victim's mind. If all the victim experienced was poverty, growing up, to them, poverty is normal and any extra money that could be saved or invested will be somehow expended just to make sure the poverty stronghold is obeyed.

THE STRONGHOLD OF POVERTY CAN ACTUALLY RESULT IN LOSS OF MONEY SO YOU GO BACK TO BEING POOR. IT BECOMES EVEN MORE DISASTROUS WHEN THE STRONGHOLD OF POVERTY HOUSES THE GENERATIONAL SPIRIT OF POVERTY. THAT COMBINATION IS DEADLY

The stronghold of poverty is like a pendulum. You can swing high and make good money for a season but the poverty stronghold will pull you back to being poor. No one can be richer than his or her mind. That poverty mindset or stronghold will always draw them down to being poor. Have you ever thought why most lottery winners die destitute? The stronghold of poverty can actually result in loss of money so you go back to being poor. It becomes even more disastrous when the stronghold of poverty houses the generational spirit of poverty. That combination is deadly.

The stronghold of poverty will cause the victim not to give because giving will make the victim rich and blessed. The victim will despise givers and abhor the rich people in church The stronghold of poverty will discourage tithing. It will suggest to the victim that you can do better with 100 % than with 90%. It hides the fact that tithing is supernatural and defies mathematical logic to prosper the tither.

To demolish this stubborn stronghold Truth must be sought. Truth that portrays the Scriptural relationship between the believer and money. Remember we have already discussed Deuteronomy 8:18 and Psalm 37:25. Psalm 65:11 also says,

"You crown the year with Your goodness, and Your paths drip with abundance."

We are encouraged, in Proverbs 3:9-10, to give so that we may have abundance. The bible says,

"Honor the Lord with your possessions, and with the firstfruits of all your increase; so your barns will be filled with plenty, and your vats will overflow with new wine."

We need money to preach the gospel. Poverty will not help us. Moreover no father wants his children poor. God, our father, is no exception. We need money here, not in heaven. There are streets of gold in heaven. We need to deal with the poverty mentality.

Remember, it was easier to get the children of Israel out of Egypt but it took God forty years, having them going in circles in the wilderness, trying to take Egypt out of them. This is why several times, they threatened to go back to Egypt. Their bodies were going to Canaan but their minds had remained in Egypt. The slavery mentality in Egypt will hinder us from getting our inheritance in the promised land. Physical and political freedom without mental freedom is no freedom at all. Christ died to make us rich. 2Corinthians 8:9 says,

"For you know the grace of our Lord Jesus Christ, that though he was rich, yet for your sake he became poor, so that you through his poverty might become rich."

PULL DOWN THE STRONGHOLD OF ANGER

CHAPTER 26

DESTROYING THE STRONGHOLD OF ANGER

This is not the anger that is part of the works of the flesh found in Galatians 5:19. Recently I listened to one of the current best players in the NBA, James Le'bron, interviewing. He grew up the only child of a single mother. They struggled a lot as he was growing up. He would see some gadgets he really wanted being advertised on TV commercials, but his mother could not afford them at the time. He said,

"Every time we couldn't afford those gadgets, anger would be bottled up in me."

This means there are a lot of people, today, who grew up in abject poverty and are angry today for not being able to afford a good life. Some are angry today for all the painful experiences they had in the journey of their lives. Some are just angry from the abusive marriages they endured for years. Some have lived with abusive families. Some are angry at how they witnessed their mothers being abused. Some suffered abuse at work. There are some who lost their jobs unfairly. The list goes on and on. Many people are angry.

This does not mean all these people are always angry. They can be very easily irritated or angered. They are not really angered by the current offense but it is coming from a deep-seated reserve of anger from their painful past. They went through episodes of events or lifestyles that stored up anger and failed to forgive and strongholds of anger were built in them.

Victims of the stronghold of anger sometimes become angry without anyone offending them. The stronghold reminds them of the pain that brought about the stored anger and they become angry. Remember the stronghold produces thoughts, that produce feelings, which will lead to actions that are commensurate to the nature of the particular stronghold. Like I have highlighted before, victims can relive, today, every year they experienced pain that caused internalized anger.

When those victims get angry sometimes they will be reliving their 10-year-old self, their 15 year old self or their 25 year old self, depending on the thought the stronghold of anger would have released. When they get mad at you, you don't even know whether you are fighting the current them or the 15 year old them or the 10 year old them. It is very unfortunate. In order to deal with the stronghold of anger, the victim needs to go back into the past and forgive and be healed of all the incidences and periods of their lives where suffering produced the anger that was stored up to become a stronghold.

This can also lead to a bipolar syndrome. They can be happy today because you meet them while they are living in their present but they can wake up angry tomorrow when the stronghold triggers thoughts of the pain from 20 years ago.

BE ENCOURAGED TO PUT DOWN THE STRONGHOLD OF ANGER, IF YOU HAPPEN TO HAVE ANY, BECAUSE IF UNDEALT WITH, IT MAY LEAD TO DEPRESSION OR TO VERY WRONG AND DISASTROUS ACTIONS

The mind needs a lot of teaching about the joy of the Lord. The victims must be encouraged to have a lot of fellowship with the Holy Spirit. He specializes in healing past wounds and He is a great help in enabling us to forgive when forgiveness is evidently difficult.

I have met victims who said,

"Pastor, I am just angry."

For such people, there is a great need for an outlet. They should be allowed to pour out their anger. If you are a counsellor allow them just to vent their anger in your counselling sessions. There are times people acted cruelly to David and we hear him in some of the Psalms venting his anger on God. He would say, for example, "Lord remember the good I did for these people and now they have set a trap for me." Pouring out your heart to God involves pouring out everything in your heart. By the way, He knows all that is in you, including your anger. After all, it's encouraging to know that giants like David also got angry and God delivered them from their anger.

Be encouraged to pull down the stronghold of anger, if you happen to have any, because if undealt with, it may lead to depression or to very wrong and disastrous actions. It can also affect the victim's public relations and cohabitability with other people. You cannot be a people person if you are angry.

CHAPTER 27

DESTROYING THE STRONGHOLD OF INSECURITY

One of the greatest sources of insecurity is when events are happening around which you feel you have no control over or you do not have absolute control. This explains why victims of this stronghold can fight hard, at any cost, by whatever means, to get to a position of control. They feel they are now secure when they are in charge. When they are in control. This happens even in some church organizations, especially those with a pyramidic structure.

Some are going to do some men-pleasing in order to climb up the ladder of control or authority. Every time a leader gets promoted by people and not by God or through men-pleasing, it weakens the office. This is because while you are in the high position God is working with you at the lower-level where, in His eyes, you deserve to be. The danger is that if that happens you are going to face wars you are not equipped to fight. You will be fighting a bishop's battle when you are equipped for an elder's battle.

Insecurity, in its quest to be in control, can cause one to fight their way up and may end up wounding others or being wounded. They end up climbing to the top by stepping on others.

It is, as a matter of fact, wise to use the energy one may use to push others down as they climb up on propelling themself up. Sometimes, because of God's love for the work of the ministry, God has a way of bringing people who carnally climb up the leadership ladder, to their rightful place they qualify to be, but usually it is a painful process. A lot of other sins will follow the victims of the stronghold of insecurity as they try to scale to the top to achieve the "supposed" security.

Sometimes, as a leader, one can see an upcoming leader doing great things and they feel threatened and become insecure. They can actually begin to ill-treat the young leader.

True security is in the Lord. He knows our future. He is the only one who has been in our past, present and future. No wonder Job says, in Job 23:10,

"But He knows the way that I take; when He has tested me, I shall come forth as gold."

Worrying about the future can cause insecurity and when the mind is constantly told that God is in control and in charge of our tomorrow, the stronghold of insecurity is pulled down.

GIVE UP PAST FAILURE

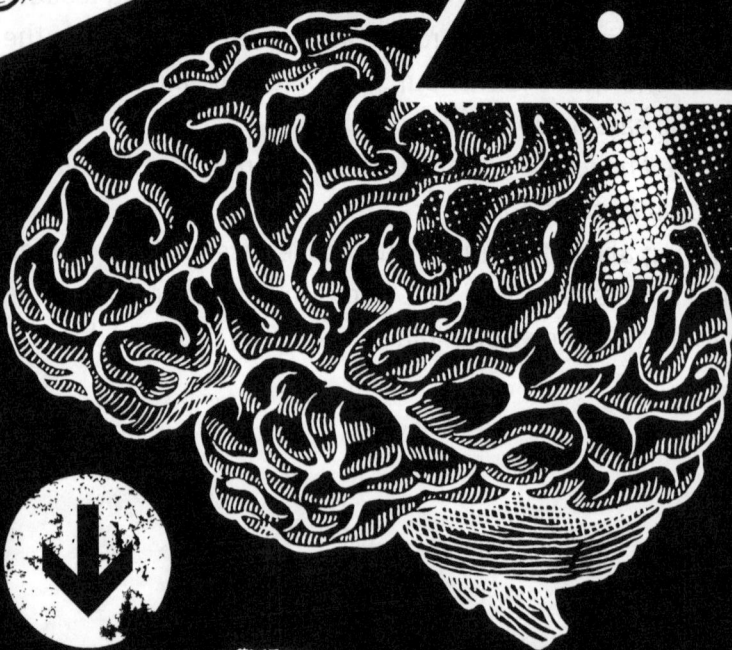

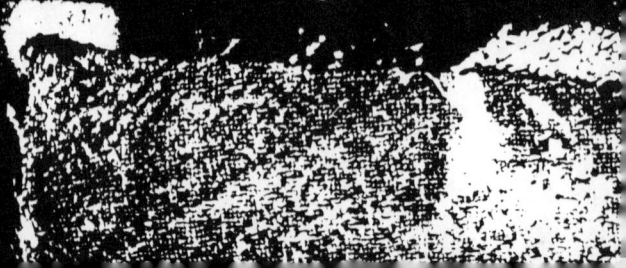

CHAPTER 28

DESTROYING THE STRONGHOLD OF PAST FAILURE

When I was in elementary school we used to sing a song that went like,

"Try, try, try again. Try, try, try again. If at first you don't succeed, try, try, try again."

Today we have Christians who behave like they've never had this song. When they fail, a stronghold is built in their minds. The lie that builds it says,

"You will never succeed again."

Because of that, they stop trying and because of that they are always scared to undertake any new venture. They become too calculative before they start anything new. Failure to handle past failure paralyses the victims for the future. Like I highlighted before, past failure can haunt a victim until he or she gets into depression. Many years ago I did a wrong investment and lost some money. Since that time every time I want to make an investment, in my mind, something says you're going to fail again. Right now I am busy pulling down that stronghold that emanated from past failure in investments.

Peter had a serious failure when he denied Jesus three times but Jesus still believed in him. When he rose from the dead, hear what the angel had to say about Peter; in Mark 16:7,

"But go, tell His disciples – and Peter – that He is going before you into Galilee; there you will see him, as He said to you."

Peter, the one who had failed greatly, denying the Master three times, is the only disciple mentioned by name. This is an indication that though Peter had failed, Jesus still had a purpose for Peter and the fact was proven by the leadership role Peter took after the Day of Pentecost.

We can still make it after failure. There is life after failure. It can still happen. I believe it. Did you know that David wrote more psalms after his failure of adultery and murder than he did before his fall. Jesus is the same yesterday, today and forever. This means he is able to deal with my past, my present and my future. The devil also specializes in condemning victims for their past failures but thank God, Jesus dealt with my past and forgave my past.

Read Daniel 3:27. The Bible has this to say about the three Hebrew young men; Shadrach, Meshach, and Abed-Nego,

"And the satraps, administrators, governors, and the king's counselors gathered together, and they saw these men on whose bodies the fire had no power; the hair of their head was not singed nor were their garments affected, and the smell of fire was not on them."

The smell of fire was not on them. When we have gone through things, when we have gone through failure, we must not smell the smoke of what we have been through. Proverbs 24:16 declares,

GOD IS THE ONLY COACH WHO CAN BEGIN WITH A TEAM OF PLAYERS WHO HAVE PAST FAILURE AND TURN THEM INTO A TEAM OF HIGH ACHIEVERS

"For a righteous man may fall seven times and rise again, but the wicked shall fall by calamity."

When I fall down there is only one way to go and that is up! When a soccer coach is hiring a player he looks at the player's resume. He must have a good record of success in that position he is being hired for. At the end the coach has a team of players full of past success. God is the only coach who can begin with a team of players who have past failure and turn them into a team of high achievers. Thank God I found a place in His team.

To pull down this stronghold, I need to tell my mind that though I failed I am not a failure. Failing does not make me a failure. Failure is not a person, it is an event.

CHAPTER 29

DESTROYING THE MINOR STRONGHOLDS

I call these minor strongholds because they are not formed over a long period of time and they are also temporal. When one is told something bad about another person, if they are not mature, a stronghold is built in their mind that sees that person as a bad person. The victim can become judgmental about the person and will begin to interpret everything the person says or does based on the stronghold that the person is bad. Even their attitude towards the person changes, all because of one lie that was told and was received.

Sometimes one can be told that his or her leader does not like them. If the victim receives that it can become a stronghold in their mind and whenever they meet that leader they feel that they don't like the leader. They begin to interpret everything the leader says or does in light of that stronghold. What the devil does is when the lie is told he orchestrates events just to confirm to you that they don't like or love you for sure.

One day I was having a chat with my spiritual mother, Apostle Eunor Guti, when we were in Jamaica. I asked her how one can be powerful in ministry and have longevity while another one will be used by God for a short time and they leave the church or become power-deficient. Her response was so deep and profound. She said,

"Sometimes the devil can tell you that your leader is bad and then he engineers events that will make you prove that it is true that the leader is really bad. As soon as you agree with that you begin to drift away in your spirit and you become powerless and you begin to lose the anointing."

This is the work of a stronghold. Never accept information which you have no proof of and if God has not spoken to you. It can become a stronghold in your mind if you do.

Someone can really offend you and mess you up. Don't conclude that they are a bad person. Anyone, including you, can also make mistakes and offend others. This will help prevent a stronghold building up in your mind about that person. This prevents you from judging them or interpreting everything that will happen afterwards based on that stronghold.

Sometimes it's about the past experiences we have had in life. My wife and I have been desiring to go on a cruise for a long time now but it has not been happening. My wife cannot imagine being on water for four days. She is not comfortable being in water. Many years ago, when she was young, she had a bad experience with water. On a bus ride from school, the bus driver tried to cross a flooded bridge and the bus slipped and hung on one wheel for hours, until they were rescued. When the last child left the bus, it fell into the flooded river with the driver only in it. From that day until now my wife does not enjoy being in water. We are busy now, trying to pull down that stronghold of fear of water.

CHAPTER 30

THE FINAL WORD

The subject of strongholds is so vast so that no single author can exhaust it in one book. We could have spoken about gambling as a stronghold. We could have discussed about food strongholds. If one can comprehend what strongholds are, how they form, and how they are pulled down, it becomes easy to tackle all the other strongholds for themself . We don't need to mention all the strongholds for you to be able to deal with them. Once you recognize that it's a stronghold, you can pull it down because I have equipped you with the weapons you need to pull down any stronghold.